THE
KENTUCKY RANGER

EDWARD T. CURNICK, A.M.

1st WORLD
LIBRARY
Literary Society

The Kentucky Ranger

Edward T. Curnick

© 1st World Library, 2007
PO Box 2211
Fairfield, IA 52556
www.1stworldlibrary.com
First Edition

LCCN: 2007930744

Softcover ISBN: 978-1-4218-4816-7
Hardcover ISBN: 978-1-4218-4719-1
eBook ISBN: 978-1-4218-4913-3

Purchase *"The Kentucky Ranger"*
as a traditional bound book at:
www.1stWorldLibrary.com/purchase.asp?ISBN=978-1-4218-4816-7

1st World Library is a literary, educational organization
dedicated to:

- Creating a free internet library of downloadable ebooks

- Hosting writing competitions and offering book publishing
  scholarships.

Interested in more 1st World Library books? contact:
literacy@1stworldlibrary.com
Check us out at: www.1stworldlibrary.com

1st World Library Literary Society

Giving Back to the World

"If you want to work on the core problem, it's early school literacy."

- James Barksdale, former CEO of Netscape

"No skill is more crucial to the future of a child, or to a democratic and prosperous society, than literacy."

- Los Angeles Times

"Literacy... means far more than learning how to read and write... The aim is to transmit... knowledge and promote social participation."

- UNESCO

"Literacy is not a luxury, it is a right and a responsibility. If our world is to meet the challenges of the twenty-first century we must harness the energy and creativity of all our citizens."

- President Bill Clinton

"Parents should be encouraged to read to their children, and teachers should be equipped with all available techniques for teaching literacy, so the varying needs and capacities of individual kids can be taken into account."

- Hugh Mackay

AUTHOR'S NOTE

The story, "The Kentucky Ranger," to a large extent is built around the life and character of one of the most famous early pioneer preachers of the West.

Many of the incidents in his career are recorded, but have been treated as to time, place and authorship according to the demands of the work with the freedom belonging to the writer of fiction.

A number of years ago some of the chapters in the narrative were printed in "The Epworth Era," of Nashville, Tennessee. Thanks are hereby extended to the paper for releasing the copyright.

CONTENTS

CHAPTER I

THE RANGER

"Glory to God! another sinner's down! Glory! Hallelujah! Amen; Pray on, brother; you'll soon be through. Glory! Glory!"

These words were shouted by two young men and a young woman who were returning through the Kentucky woods from a camp meeting. They were riding in a smart spring wagon drawn by two good horses. The young man who was not driving would fall into the wagon, crying for mercy, and the driver shouted: "Glory to God! another sinner's down!" and the young lady added: "Keep on praying, brother; you'll soon be saved. Glory! Glory to God!" Then the young men would change places, and the other would shout: "You'll soon get through, brother; pray on. Glory!"

These persons acted thus to tantalize a camp meeting preacher who was riding on horseback ahead of them. He detected their mockery and tried to outride them; but his horse being somewhat lame he could not escape them.

The preacher remembered that at a little distance beyond the road ran through a swamp but that a bridle path wound around it. Putting spurs to his horse he made for this path but the driver, keeping on the road, whipped up his horses. Driving into the swamp in his haste and excitement he did not notice a stump at the side of the road. Crash! went the fore wheel against the stump, and mounting to its top over went the wagon into the mud and water. The two young men took a flying leap into the swamp, and the young lady was thrown out. She was almost smothered before she was rescued by the young men. While they were in this predicament the preacher rode up to the edge of the morass. Raising himself in his stirrups he shouted at the top of his voice: "Glory to God! Glory to God! another sinner's down! Hallelujah! Glory! Glory!" Then he added: "Now you poor, miserable sinners, take this as a judgment from God upon you for your meanness, and repent of your wicked ways before it is too late." With this he left them, covered with mud and shame, to their reflections.

Jasper Very (for this was the preacher's name) continued on his way, now laughing at the sorry plight of his mockers, again singing a hymn with such power that the leaves of the trees seemed to tremble with the melody, and anon lifting his heart in prayer to his Maker. The object of his ride through the woods was to visit a settler who a short time before had been caught by a falling tree and suffered the fracture of his leg. The man of God brought the consolations of religion to the injured man and his family. After partaking of their plain but hospitable fare, he went to the barn for his faithful horse. While he is preparing to mount him we shall attempt to describe this backwoods preacher's appearance.

We see at once that he is a splendid type of Kentucky manhood. He stands six feet two inches in his heavy rawhide boots, but his frame is so well proportioned that he does not seem so tall. His head is massive and his hair as thick and disheveled as a lion's mane; it cannot be kept in order. His eyes are dark blue, and can twinkle with merriment or blaze

Edward T. Curnick

with indignation. His mouth is of medium size, mobile, yet strong; when closed the drooping corners give the face a set expression. Great firmness and decision are shown by the broad but rounded chin, which forms a base for a smooth-shaven countenance. His frame is large and powerful and is overlaid with muscles hard as iron and elastic as steel. His hands are large and have a Samsonlike grip in them. A long coat of homespun cloth is well fitted to his body, with waistcoat and trousers of the same material. A black stock loosely tied about his neck sets off a white shirt of coarse linen. His whole make-up gives one the impression of fearlessness, determination and energy, mixed with gentle-ness, kindness and charity. Humor shines in his face like heat lightning in a summer cloud.

Jasper Very's parents were pioneers from the State of Virginia. Hearing of the fertility and beauty of Kentucky they, like many others, decided to emigrate to that land of promise. In 1785 they, with their infant son Jasper, started out to brave the perils of the wilderness. Perils there were in plenty. Kentucky at that time was the scene of repeated Indian raids, ambuscades, burning of homes, scalpings, and other atrocities. The Red Man was determined that his choicest Hunting Ground should not be possessed by the White Man. The Indians were met by such hardy and invincible scouts and frontiersmen as Daniel Boone, Simon Kenton and George Rogers Clark. For years the conflict was carried on until finally the savages were driven out of the state and its marvelous valleys and hills were left to the white man there to fulfil his destiny as the aborigines had theirs before him. The Very family escaped the horrors of battle, massacre and captivity. They settled on a site of great natural beauty in Lincoln County, near the Tennessee line.

While the physical surroundings of the Verys were fairly entrancing, we are sorry to confess that the moral environment was anything but elevating and desirable. In fact the neighborhood was considered one of the worst in all the newly settled country. It received the name of Rogues' Harbor and well deserved the title. Many of the settlers had committed crimes in the Eastern States and had fled to the wilderness to escape punishment. They composed a majority of the people of the district, and when arrested for breaking the law swore one another clear in the courts of justice. At last the respectable people combined for their own protection in an organization called the Regulators. Several bloody encounters took place between the Regulators and the outlaws before order was established in the community.

Jasper Very was a lively youngster from the start, and surely Rogues' Harbor was not the best place in which to bring up a vigorous and vivacious boy. He early showed elements of power and leadership, having a remarkably strong and well developed body, being a stranger to fear, a wit and a wag, and loving the rude sports and pastimes of the period. Apart from the home there were few opportunities for mental or religious training. Schools were few and scarcely worthy of the name. No newspapers were published in that section. Sunday was a day set apart for hunting, fishing, horse-racing, card-playing, dancing and other amusements.

It is little wonder that Jasper became a wild and wicked boy. He was a leader among his fellows in the rough sports of the time. His father gave him a race-horse and he became renowned among his companions for fearless riding. At card-playing he was skillful and lucky. But Jasper had one blessed, restraining influence which doubtless kept him from going the full course of sin and folly—a devout, humble, praying, Christian mother.

Happy the boy who in the slippery paths of youth can lean upon the loving arm of a godly mother.

Edward T. Curnick

When sixteen years of age Jasper experienced a great change of heart and conduct. It was the turning point of his life. With his father and brother he attended a wedding in the neighborhood. With others he took part in the uproarious merriment of the occasion. Returning home he began to think of his wicked ways, and at once felt condemned. His mind became so agitated that his body was affected. His heart palpitated in a very violent manner, his sight left him, and he thought death was at hand. Very sure was he that he was not prepared to die. Falling on his knees he cried to God to have mercy on his soul. Though it was late at night his mother heard his cries, sprang from her bed, and was soon at his side praying for her son, and exhorting him to look to Christ for mercy. They prayed together a long time, and little sleep came to them that night. Jasper resolved from that time to be a Christian. He asked his father to sell the racehorse, and gave his pack of cards to his mother, who threw them into the fire.

However, it was many days before Jasper really felt that he was converted. Finally he found peace of mind at a camp meeting. We quote from a record of his experience: "On the Saturday evening of said meeting I went with weeping multitudes, bowed before the sand, and earnestly prayed for mercy. In the midst of a solemn struggle of soul an impression was made on my mind as though a voice said to me: 'Thy sins are all forgiven thee.' Divine light flashed all around me, unspeakable joy sprang up in my soul. I rose to my feet, opened my eyes, and it really seemed as if I were in heaven; the trees, the leaves on them, and every thing seemed to be, and I really thought were, praising God. My mother raised a shout, my Christian friends crowded around me and joined me in praising God—I have never doubted that the Lord did then and there forgive my sins and gave me religion." He went on his way rejoicing, and before he reached his majority became a backwoods preacher. He had been ranging over the hills and valleys of Kentucky for four years, preaching the gospel in many places, when he is introduced to our readers.

Jasper Very was known early in his ministry as a great camp meeting preacher. He was always partial to such gatherings, partly because at one of them he had found religion. These meetings in the woods, "God's first temples," are of enough importance to merit description in another chapter.

Edward T. Curnick

CHAPTER II

AN OLD TIME CAMP MEETING

To Kentucky belongs the honor of originating the modern camp meeting. This is no small distinction, when we consider how these institutions have spread over the land and the great good they have done. Camp meetings grew out of the needs of the times. When they providentially sprang up in Kentucky, the frontier was sparsely settled, most people living miles away from any church. Such churches as were built were small and could accommodate only a few persons, and preaching services were often weeks apart.

The revivals of genuine religion which usually attended these gatherings were much needed in the backwoods. Most of the settlers were honest, law-abiding persons, who had sought to improve their means by emigrating to this western country; but many of the vicious off-scouring of the older settlements also went west to hide their crimes or to commit new ones. Rogues' Harbor was only an extreme type of many law-defying places. Murderers, thieves, gamblers, defaulters and their kind put life in peril, and threatened the moral and social order of the state. These camp meetings strengthened and encouraged good people, reformed many bad men and women, and thus became a saving leaven of righteousness.

And what a place for a camp meeting was the Kentucky forest. What nature poet can do justice to such sylvan loveliness as we find in the "Blue Grass Region?" The pen must be dipped in the juices of that Edenic vegetation and tinted with the blue of that arching sky to record such beauty. What stately trees! They seemed like pillars in God's own temple. The rich, warm limestone soil gave birth to trees in form and variety scarce equaled in the world. Here grew in friendly fellowship and rivalry the elm, ash, hickory, walnut, wild cherry, white, black and read oak, black and honey locust, and many others. Their lofty branches interlocking formed a verdant roof which did not entirely shut out the sun's rays but caused a light subdued and impressive as the light in a Saint Paul's Cathedral.

In such a forest was pitched the camp to which Jasper Very returned. Let me describe this old-fashioned camp ground. A large, rough shed was erected, capable of protecting five thousand persons from wind and rain. It was covered with clapboards and furnished with puncheon seats. At one end a large stand was built, from which sermons were preached. A few feet in front of this stand a plain altar rail was set, extending the full length of the preachers' stand. This altar was called the "mourners' bench." All around the altar a liberal supply of fresh straw was placed upon which the worshippers knelt. On three sides of the large shed camps or cabins of logs were built for the use of the attendants. In the rear of the preachers' stand was a large room which accommodated all the ministers who labored in the meeting. The effect at the camp at night was very striking. At intervals of several rods log fires were kept burning and the bright light they threw was contrasted with the deep darkness beyond.

It is astonishing to read how great an attraction these camps became to the hardy pioneers of the Kentucky wilderness.

Edward T. Curnick

People gathered from all quarters in all kinds of vehicles, some traveling thirty or forty miles. Many came in covered wagons in which they slept at night. History records, that at Cane Ridge, Kentucky, a camp meeting was held attended by twenty thousand people.

It is ten o'clock Sunday morning at Oak Grove Camp Meeting, where our hero Jasper Very is laboring. Thousands are in the great wooden structure, filling every seat and standing many deep beyond the edges of the building. The preachers' stand contains twenty-five or thirty ministers gathered from many parts of the State. The crowd has even overflowed this stand, and all available room is occupied.

The Christians present have been prepared for this service by the cabin meetings held at six o'clock in the morning and a prayer and testimony meeting in the tabernacle at eight. And now the service begins. A stalwart son of the prophets arises and announces the hymn:

"Come, sinners, to the gospel feast,
Let every soul be Jesus' guest:
There need not one be left behind,
For God hath bidden all mankind."

He starts the first note, and thousands take up the inspiring strain, and the glorious music rolls through the forest like the sound of many waters. A passage of Scripture is read and a fervent prayer offered. A second hymn is sung: "There is a fountain filled with blood," and far away the cadence is heard rising and falling, thrilling waves of sound.

The song is ended. A rustling noise is heard as the people settle themselves in their places, and then a deep quiet ensues as they look expectantly toward the preachers' stand. One whispers to another: "Who is to be the preacher this morning?" They are not left long in doubt. Slowly the minister arises. It is Jasper Very, the star preacher of the camp meeting. He comes before his audience with a humble self-possession which is reflected in the composure of his face. How did he obtain this self-possession? Reader, we must lift the veil somewhat and let you see.

In the morning he had gone into the deep woods to study and pray, as was the wont of the forest preachers. Here he had prayerfully and carefully completed the outline of his sermon. Then a great burden of unfitness and helplessness came upon him. Like his Master he threw himself prone upon the ground and poured out his soul to the Father. "O God," he cried, "who am I, that I should be thy ambassador to beseech sinners to be reconciled to thee? Who am I that I should stand between the living and the dead and offer life and immortality to men? Thou, O God, only art my suffi-ciency, my hope, my expectation. Stand by my side and help me in this hour, for my need is great. This I ask in the name of thy Son Jesus Christ. Amen."

Coming thus from the hidings of divine power, with the Spirit of God like dew resting upon him, he announces his text: "Seek ye the Lord while he may be found, call ye upon him while he is near: let the wicked forsake his way, and the unrighteous man his thoughts: and let him return unto the Lord, and he will have mercy upon him; and to our God, for he will abundantly pardon."

He began by describing the way of the wicked. He unmasked sin, showing its hideous deformity, how it pollutes the soul, and makes man unfit for fellowship with a holy God. Then he passed on to show the guilt of sin, the awful misery coming to a man when he is face to face with his iniquities. With great skill he pointed out condemnation arising from particular transgressions,—the defaulter fleeing from his

Edward T. Curnick

country, the murderer with his victim's bloody form ever before his mind's eye, the lustful man tortured and consumed with the rewards of his own folly. Continuing, he proceeded to tell the final punishment of these sinners. In those days ministers at camp meetings preached a literal hell; and as the speaker uncovered the pit of destruction and compelled his hearers to look into it many felt that they were "hair hung and breeze shaken" over the mouth of perdition.

Now his manner changed. His voice, instead of being loud and startling like thunder, producing awe and terror, became sweet, tender, and appealing, like a shepherd calling his sheep to the fold.

Having opened the wounds of sin, he poured into them the cordial of gospel grace. He dwelt upon the words, "abundantly pardon," showing how God had planned to put away sin by the gift of his Son and had promised forgiveness to all guilty mortals who with hearty repentance and true faith looked to Christ for salvation.

As he exalted the world's Redeemer from one plane to another his soul was lifted up with indescribable joy and exultation. His voice and form were in attune with his soul. We have read that this man's voice could be heard a mile, and on this occasion it surely reached to the utmost bounds of that great assembly. Extending his arms, as though he would enfold the multitude and present them to the Savior, he besought sinners to flee from impending wrath, to come to the altar and be saved from sin so that they might "read their titles clear to mansions in the skies."

The effect was tremendous. At once a rush was made for the mourners' bench and it was soon filled. Many were stricken where they sat in the congregation and fell on their knees imploring mercy. Around the mourners gathered the saints of

God, counseling, advising, quoting suitable passages of Scripture, praying with the penitents. When the meeting finally closed long after the dinner hour, scores professed conversion, and a great victory for morality and religion in Kentucky had been won.

Edward T. Curnick

CHAPTER III

SWAPPING STORIES

The ministers were in the preachers' room on the afternoon of this camp meeting day. They were scattered about in delightful abandon. Some had thrown themselves on rough cots; others were lounging on rude benches which served as seats; the few plain chairs which the place boasted were also occupied. Most of the men were regaling themselves with the fragrant Kentucky tobacco, and the blue smoke ascended in widening spirals to the rafters above. They felt they must unbend after the severe mental tension of the morning.

What a fine spirit of comradeship is found among a group of preachers of one heart and mind. Can anything on earth surpass it? Here we find the hearty handshake, the contagious laugh, faces bright with smiles, a free flow of talk. We see hilarity without vulgarity, wit that sparkles, but does not burn, as when a bright sally directed at some brother's foibles is met with a quick repartee. We listen to anecdotes which cheer and enliven the senses without hurting the conscience or debasing the mind.

"Brother Larkin, give us a bit of wit or philosophy from 'Poor Richard' or tell us one of your good anecdotes."

The man addressed was John Larkin. He was about thirty-five years old and was known as the "square man" both as to body and mind. His head seemed more square than round, and was set upon a strong neck which rested upon square shoulders. From shoulders to the ground he was in the form of a parallelogram. His hands were wide and short, the fingers being of nearly equal length, giving the hands a blunt, square appearance. His gray eyes were wide apart, having a sly and merry cast in them, while crow lines in their corners gave them a laughing expression. His firm mouth and square chin showed that he could mingle seriousness with mirth. He was considerably under the average height, but thickset and strong.

John Larkin was of New England descent. When a small boy he had moved with his parents from "'way down East" to far-famed Kentucky. There he helped his father clear the wilderness and make a comfortable home. At twenty-three years of age he was powerfully converted, and soon after became a traveling preacher.

John had stored his mind with the homely proverbs of Benjamin Franklin and many bright sayings of other writers. He saw the ludicrous side of things and was fond of telling anecdotes. Hence the request which a brother minister made of him.

"About two months ago," said Larkin, "I had an appointment to preach in a private house. The boys of the family had a pet sheep which they had taught to butt. Going near him, they would make motions with their heads, and the sheep would back out and dart forward at the boys; but they would jump aside and so escape. A drunken man came into the congregation and sat on the end of a bench near the door. He had caroused the whole night before and presently began to nod. As he nodded and bent forward, the sheep came along by the door and seeing the man moving his head up and down, took it as a banter and backed and then sprang forward, and gave the sleeper a severe jolt right on the head, and over he tilted him. The whole congregation laughed outright and I joined in with them."

The preachers laughed at the story as heartily as those who saw the occurrence. One stout parson remarked: "The tipsy man surely was the butt of that joke." A clergyman from down Cumberland River way said: "I hope the sheep knocked drunkenness out of him and common sense and decency into him."

Larkin, his face wreathed in smiles, turned to a great strapping Kentuckian, and said: "Now Brother Harvey, let us hear from you."

The man addressed was well known by the company. Naturally strong he grew up on a farm, where his out-of-doors life added to temperate habits gave him a finely developed body. He lived with his wife and five grown up children on a splendid quarter section of land bordering on the Cumberland River. He was a lay preacher, cultivating his farm week days and preaching on Sunday.

"Well, brethren," began David Harvey, "I could tell you stories of wild Indians, panthers and wild cats that I saw in my youth, and some tolerably trying experiences I have been through since becoming a preacher, but today I am going to repeat a tale I heard not long ago concerning Jasper Very. He seems comfortable there sitting on one bench with his feet on another, and if my story lacks anything he can supply the missing links.

"Brother Very was attending a camp meeting in the edge of Tennessee when an incident of thrilling interest occurred.

Two young men, distantly related, sons of respectable and wealthy parents, lived in the settlement. They were both paying attention to a very wealthy young lady. Soon a rivalship for her hand sprang up between them, which created a bitter jealousy in the heart of each. After quarreling and fighting they both armed themselves, and each bound himself by a solemn oath to kill the other. Armed with pistols and dirks they attended the camp meeting. Brother Very was acquainted with the young men, and had been told of the unfortunate affair. On Sunday he was preaching to a large congregation on the terrors of the law. Many fell under the preaching of the word. He called for mourners to come to the altar and the two young men, deeply convicted of sin, came and knelt before God. One entered on the right and the other on the left, each being ignorant of the act of the other. The preacher went deliberately to each of them, took their deadly weapons from their bosoms, and carried them into the preachers' room. Returning he labored faithfully with them and others nearly all the afternoon and night. These young men cried hard for mercy, and while he was kneeling by the side of one of them, just before the break of day, the Lord spake peace to his soul. He arose, and gave some thrilling shouts. Jasper then hurried to the other young man, at the other side of the altar, and he was saved in less than fifteen minutes and, standing upright, shouted victory. As these young men faced about they saw each other, and starting simultaneously, met about midway of the altar, and instantly clasped each other in their arms. What a shout went up to heaven that night from these young men, and from almost all the number present."

This narrative strongly affected the group of ministers, and some more emotional than others shouted: "Praise the Lord! Hallelujah!"

"Brother Very, did I tell the story right?" said Harvey.

Edward T. Curnick

"You told it about as it was," responded Very, "only there is this sequel to add: one of these young men made an able and successful preacher. After traveling a few years his health failed, and he died triumphantly."

A sallow-faced parson from the river-bottoms remarked: "Jasper Very has been through many trying experiences, and I am going to ask him to tell us how he conquered that cantankerous woman by tact and muscles."

Thus appealed to, Very told the following anecdote: "Some time ago I crossed the Ohio River into the State of Illinois where I had some preaching engagements. On one of my tours I met a local preacher who was a small, good natured, pious and withal a useful preacher. He had a wife who was a noted virago. She was high tempered, overbearing and quarrelsome. She opposed her husband's preaching, and was unwilling he should ask a blessing at the table or conduct family prayers. If he persisted in his effort to pray she would run noisily about the rooms and overturn the chairs. If unable to stop him any other way she would catch a cat and throw it in his face while he was kneeling and trying to pray. The little man had invited several preachers to his home to talk with the woman and bring her to a better frame of mind, but she cursed them to their face and raged like one possessed. Several times he invited me to go home with him, but I was afraid to trust myself. I pitied the poor little man so much that finally I yielded, and went home with him one evening. When we arrived I saw she was mad, and the devil was in her as big as an alligator. So I determined on my course. After supper her husband said very kindly: 'Come, wife, stop your little affairs, and let us have prayers.' To this she replied: 'I will have none of your praying about me.' Speaking mildly, I expostulated with her, but to no use; for the longer I spoke the more wrathful she became, and she cursed me most bitterly. Then I spoke sternly and said:

'Madam, if you were a wife of mine, I would break you of your bad ways, or I would break your neck.'

"'The devil you would!' she said. With this she poured upon me such a torrent of curses as was almost beyond endurance."

"'Be still,' said I, 'we must and will have prayer.' Again she declared we should not."

'Now,' I remarked to her, 'if you do not be still, and behave yourself, I'll put you out of doors.' At this she clenched her fist, swore at me, and told me I could not put her out. I caught her by the arm, and swinging her round in a circle brought her up to the cabin door, and shoved her out. She jumped up, tore her hair, foamed, all the time swearing in a terrible way. The door was made very strong to keep out hostile Indians. I shut it tightly, barred it, and went to prayer. Under such conditions praying was difficult, I assure you, but I was determined to conquer or die.

"While she was raging, foaming and roaring on the outside I was singing with a loud voice spiritual hymns on the inside to drown her words as much as possible. At last she became perfectly exhausted and panted for breath. Then she became calm and still, and knocking at the door said: 'Mr. Very, please let me in.'"

"'Will you behave yourself, if I let you in?' said I."

"'O yes,' replied she, 'I will.' With this I opened the door, took her by the hand, led her in, and seated her by the fire-place. She was in a high perspiration, and looked pale as death. After she was seated she said: 'What a fool I am.' 'Yes,' said I, 'about one of the biggest fools I ever saw in my life. Now, you have to repent of all this or your soul will be

Edward T. Curnick

lost.' She sat silent, and I said 'Brother C., let us pray again.' We kneeled down and both prayed. His wife was as quiet as a lamb. And what is better, in less than six months this woman was soundly converted, and became as bold in the cause of God as she had been in the cause of the wicked one.'"

CHAPTER IV

THE TRAIL OF THE SERPENT

While these ministers of grace were engaged in pleasant conversation a different kind of a crowd had met not far away. They were moonshiners. Their rendezvous was a cave near the top of a hill about one mile back from the Cumberland River. A motley company of about a dozen men they were, dressed in cheap trousers supported by "galluses," coarse shirts, and wide-brim straw hats.

Sam Wiles was leader of this band. As these pages are often to be burdened with his name, we shall now take his measure. He belonged to that part of the population called "poor whites." His parents had come to the settlement when Sam was a little boy. They were poor, shiftless, improvident, ignorant, and, worse than all, apparently contented with their lot. They dwelt in a log cabin in the hills, and in a haphazard way cultivated a few acres of half-barren land, raising a little corn, tobacco, hay, fruit, and a few vegetables. There were six children in the family, of whom Sam was the oldest. Five dogs guarded the house and helped to make the inmates poor. "Tige," the coon dog, was the favorite of this quintette.

Sam Wiles was the brightest of the children, his mind being naturally active; but he had little disposition for study and

Edward T. Curnick

very meager opportunities, for "school kept" only a few weeks in a year. At the time of this story he had just passed his majority, was somewhat above medium height, solidly built, with broad, square shoulders. His brown hair hung several inches below a coonskin cap he wore, and was supplemented by a large mustache of which he was very proud.

Behold this leader of the moonshiners as he stirs the fire of logs under the still and speaks to his pals:

"That war a mighty fine trick I played on Dick Granger, the revenue deputy t'other night. He was after me with his dorgs, and saw me as I was crossin' the road near Franklin Schoolhouse. 'Halt, there!' he hollored; but I was not in the haltin' bizness, and I made tracks fur Pigeon Crick close by. As I run he fired off his gun; but the light was dim and I was mighty peart, and dodged in time. He called to his bloodhounds and said, 'Sic 'im, Rex; ketch 'im Bull,' but by that time I was wadin' in the crick. I run 'long till I cum to that big white oak which grows by the crick where it makes a turn north, and I jumped and caught a big branch an' pulled myself up into the tree. Then I walked on the thick branches till I got to the furder side, and there war standin' by the oak a mighty fine sugar maple with branches which touched the oak. I walked out on an oak branch as fur as I could go, and then swung from my hands back and for'ard with all my might. At last my feet touched a branch and letting go my hands, I swung down like a ham of meat in a smokehouse. Soon I pulled myself up and made fifty feet crossing that tree, and then I dun the same turn to a big walnut tree; and so on till I knew the dorgs could not track me, when I clim down to the ground and got safe back to the cave."

"That war a monkey trick, shore nuff," said Tom Walker, a gaunt fellow over six feet tall, who was stretched on the ground by the fire, and who, because of his height, was usually called "Long Tom." In his cavernous mouth he held an immense chew of tobacco, and ever and anon he squirted tobacco juice into the fire with a precision and force which showed long practice.

"I wish the devil would kill the whole crew of revenue officers," said Wiles. "Why should we be hunted like wild beasts for makin' a few gallons of whisky? Do we not raise the corn, and have we not a right to turn it into drink? You fellers know how hard it is to make a living on these hills; and if we make more money by changing corn into whisky, why should we be hindered and our lives put into danger? We have a right to make whisky and to drink it and to sell it, and I'm goin' to do it in spite of all the officers in Kentucky," and he brought his big fist down with a thwack on his knee to give emphasis to his words.[1]

[1] It was impossible for this lawbreaker to foresee that in about one hundred years the whole whisky business in its beverage aspects would be prohibited by law in the United States, and that the sophistry he used would be employed by multitudes in denying the eighteenth amendment to the national constitution.

"Now yer speaking the truth, pardner," drawled Long Tom as he ejected from his mouth a generous quantity of tobacco juice. "My father fit in the Revolutionary War for liberty 'way down in ole Virginy, and I'll never submit to have my right to make home-distilled whisky taken away."

"Always stick to that and you'uns will be a man, even if you'uns die with yer boots on."

The speaker was Zibe Turner, a creature who would pass for a Calaban. A monster he was except his legs, which were short and slim, giving him a dwarfish appearance. So he was a monster dwarf, if such a term is allowable. His head was immense in size, covered with long unkempt hair. His shoulders, arms and trunk would become a giant. A look at his face showed a low forehead, black, restless eyes, wide apart, flat nose, and large mouth.

Like Calaban he could be called "hag-seed," or the son of a witch and a devil.

His moral nature was as misshapen as his body. His mind was degraded, yet keen in plotting mischief and violence. His affections were debased. Prospero's description of Calaban applied to him:

"Abhorred slave which any print of goodness will not take Being capable of all ill."

The words of Saint Paul to the sorcerer fitted him: "O full of all subtlety and all mischief, thou child of the devil, thou enemy of all righteousness." He was a type of those whom the apostle described as "filled with all unrighteousness, fornication, wickedness, covetousness, maliciousness; full of envy, murder, deceit, malignity—implicable, unmerciful."

Strangely enough, one of the moonshiners had read Shakespeare's "Tempest," and gave Caliban's title of "monster" to Zibe Turner. From that day he was generally nicknamed "Monster Turner."

"Always stick to dat," repeated Turner in his deep, gutteral voice. "Let's drink to de health of all moonshiners and to de defeat an' death of all revenue spies. Dat's my holt (hold)." Suiting the action to the words, he raised a stone jug nearly full of spirits to his lips and taking a long draught, handed it to the next, and so it went the rounds. The liquor, which would have made an ordinary drinker intoxicated in a few minutes, had no perceptible effect upon these men, who scarcely ever tasted water, so commonly did they drink the product of their stills; but it perhaps raised their feelings a trifle and loosened their tongues to speak other words and strengthened their purposes to perform unlawful acts.

Sam Wiles then spoke: "Next to these officer dorgs who hunt us on the hills and mountains, I hate them shoutin' hypercrits who air holdin' that camp meetin' near Poplar Crick. They're tryin' to make the whul county pious, and you fellers know how their head men have jined with others around here to appint a vigilance committee to drive all such as we'uns air out'n the State. Because we believe in pursonal liberty, because we think it right to make our own whisky and to race our hosses, because we sometimes try our luck at cards and win money from the young fools in the valley, they want to put the law on our tracks. Now the more camp meetin's we have around here, the less pursonal liberty we shall have; and I propose to you'ns that we jine with the boys on Honey Crick and bust up the camp meetin'."

This proposition was hailed with delight by all the company except Long Tom. When he had cleared his mouth of juice, he drawled out: "Byes, none of ye would like to see that meetin' capsized better nor I would. But we must be sure of our ground. I have hearn that the star preacher there—what's his name? Jasper Hurry? No. Very? That's it, Jasper Very. I have hearn that he is almighty strong and brave, and we had better be keerful how we tackle 'im."

"Shucks," said Wiles, "they air all cowards, and their magistrates will run at the first attack; and I say it is to our interest to break up that meetin', and do it right away. What do you say, byes?"

Edward T. Curnick

They all consented to the attack, and took another swig around from the big jug to seal the agreement.

"Now," said their leader, "it's time you'ns went to yer homes. Zibe Turner will stay, and we'uns will tend de fire. Long Tom, tomorrow you go to Bert Danks, the captain of the Honey Crick crowd, and ask him and his pals to meet us here in de evenin'."

CHAPTER V

ROWDIES IN CAMP

Sam Wiles and Zibe Turner attended to the still while the day began to wane, and shadows cast by the tall hills were lengthening over the plain.

When darkness finally came Wiles continued to replenish the fire and supply the necessary water from a running stream. His boon companion threw himself down on some cedar boughs within the cave's mouth and was soon asleep. His watch would come later on.

While this precious pair of "wildcatters" are thus employed, a good opportunity is given us to describe their retreat.

Their rendezvous was called Wind Cave, and was discovered a few years before by a young brother of Sam Wiles. The boy, Ephraim Wiles, one day was hunting stray cattle on some hills skirting the Cumberlands River, when he came to the top of a hill which was nearly bare of timber and whose southern side was a sheer perpendicular of rock for several feet down. The boy stood looking over this precipice, lost his footing, and fell down the cliff. He was unhurt, for about fifteen feet below was a level place a few feet across covered with leaves and moss and upon this he landed. When he had

Edward T. Curnick

recovered from his surprise, he looked about him and saw that the hillside below him was very steep, with trees and bushes growing thickly in the soil. Then he turned his eyes toward the rock, and beheld an aperture of considerable size partly covered by bushes and decayed vegetation. With a boy's curiosity and daring he crawled into the opening, and found himself in a cave of moderate dimensions. Finding in it nothing but broken rocks and white walls and a small stream of water flowing along, he soon crept out, and knowing no way of escape save down the hill side, slipped over the edge, and by holding on to bushes and shrubs and checking himself against trunks of trees he finally reached the bottom, and, returning home, told of his discovery to the family.

From this time the cave became the resort of Sam Wiles and his moonshiners, and here they carried on their illicit distilling with little fear of detection. They explored its interior thoroughly, and discovered that the cave went north for a considerable distance, when it turned to the east, its dimensions becoming narrower as they proceeded. At last they came to a second entrance which opened upon the hill's side about midway between top and bottom. This aperture was partially close by fallen logs and decayed leaves and mold. The two openings made the cave a sort of tunnel, and because there was always a current of air passing through the passages they named it "Wind Cave." The narrow entrance was used for receiving sacks of corn, barrels, and other necessaries of their unlawful work, and also for removing the whisky after it had been made. The men kept this hole well secured by covering it with brush. As the other part of the cave was much larger, it was there that the still was set up, and there the outlaws usually remained.

Behold them this Saturday evening brewing mischief as well as distilling whisky. They were a reckless, religion-hating crowd. They were mostly young men, though some had passed middle life. Nearly all were shabbily dressed, and of large and bony frame. The faces of most were heavy and dull showing marks of dissipation. Others, especially the very young men, were really fine specimens of Kentucky physical manhood. They had rosy cheeks, bright eyes, and a ready smile and laugh. Surely they were worthy of a better cause.

In a way they were as jolly and hearty, as full of fun and jokes, as the ministers themselves. Their conversation was coarse and marred the King's English; it was boisterous and narrow, but it fitted their characters.

They were seated on logs or on the moss-covered ground in or near the cave's mouth. Each one was smoking a corncob pipe or rolling a quid of tobacco under his tongues.

These men had no compunctions of conscience either as to the lawlessness of their business, or to their desire and will to disturb the peace of the camp meeting. Sam Wiles speaks: "Fellers, tomorrer is Sunday, and we'uns must spile their meetin' on de camp ground. You'ns must arm yo'selves with any weapons you'ns can git—dirks, knives, clubs, and horse-whips. You'ns, Long Tom and Bert Banks, will walk right into de crowd while de preacher is spoutin' and start to break up de meetin'. De rest of you'ns must be ready to help."

"Right you air," said Bert Danks, captain of the Honey Crick band. "Long Tom and I will go, and I 'low all we'uns can make a rip-roarin' time, for we'll frighten de people, and be too much for de preachers and magistrates. I'll bring a passel of my bully byes with me, and they'll make things lively at de camp."

Long Tom remained silent, but a close observer might have seen a look on his face telling that his part of the program was not exactly agreeable, but he was not a man to shirk a hard task.

"Won't I laugh to hear de women scream and to see 'em run over benches like scart sheep," said Monster Turner. "You'ns will have to be right smart to keep up with me on de camp ground, for I'm goin' to have my fightin' clothes on from hat to boots. Confound 'em, dose pesky preachers won't fight, and we'll be too many for de officers. Dat's my holt."

These words wrought the men up to a higher pitch of excitement, and Wiles their leader, wishing still further to work on their feelings, said to Lem Curtis, a blue eyed youth of eighteen:

"Lem, you air de best singer in de bunch, and I want you to lead us in our favorite song. No revenues air near tonight, and we'uns air safe from danger if we'uns do not sing too loud."

Thus appealed to, Lem Curtis started a well known refrain, the rest joining in heartily.

After all had paid their respects to the brown jug Sam Wiles dismissed the meeting with these words: "We'uns shall meet near de edge of de camp on de east at seven o'clock tomorrer mornin', an' all you fellers be shore to be in time."

Sunday morning dawned beautiful and bright. The numbers on the camp ground were constantly being increased by persons coming on horseback, in buggies, wagons, and every known vehicles. Jasper Very was the preacher at ten o'clock. Everything proceeded in a becoming manner until he was half through his discourse, when up stalked near to the stand Bert Danks and Long Tom with hats on and loaded whips in their hands. They remained standing, and began talking in an audible voice with some women of their acquaintance. Naturally many eyes were turned to this scene, and the attention given to the speaker was lost.

Jasper Very stopped in his sermon and, turning to the rowdies, said: "Young men, this is a religious meeting, held by Christian people, and protected by the laws of Kentucky. You will therefore get down off those benches, cease from talking, and be quiet and orderly."

Instead of complying with this request, both of the rowdies cursed the preacher, and said: "You'ns mind yer own bizness. We'uns will not get down from dese seats."

Jasper knew that trouble was present, and being sure that it was vain to continue preaching, he cried out: "I call for the magistrates on this ground to come forward and take these men into custody." There were several officers at hand; but they, being afraid, declared they could not arrest them.

Jasper spoke to them: "Command me to take them, and I will do it at the risk of my life." Saying this, he advanced toward them. "Stand off," shouted both of the rowdies; but the preacher walked forward, when Bert Danks struck at him with his loaded whip, but that moment Jasper seized him and jerked him off the bench. A regular scuffle ensued, and the congregation was in great commotion. The magistrates, having found their courage, commanded all friends of order to aid in suppressing the riot. By this time Jasper Very had thrown Bert Danks down and, despite his utmost efforts to arise, held him fast. About the same instant two lusty farmers who were standing by the preacher took hold of Long Tom and bore him to the ground.

Then the mob headed by Sam Wiles and Monster Turner with loud outcries rushed to the rescue of the prisoners. They

Edward T. Curnick

knocked down seven magistrates and several preachers and many others. At this point Jasper Very gave his prisoner to others, and threw himself in front of the order-loving people. At once Sam Wiles confronted him. His eyes were blazing with bitter hate. His rage was so great that it weakened his judgment, and he struck out again and again at Very to fell him. The last time he struck at him the momentum threw the side of his face toward the preacher. It was too great a temptation to resist and Jasper hit him a sudden and powerful blow in the ear which dropped him to the earth.

Meantime the fight was waxing fierce in another direction. Zibe Turner led a part of the mob to the right of the fighting, and attempted a flank movement. He seemed like a personification of Satan. His black eyes glared with a terrible fury, and with his long arms outstretched he rushed on the fray. His voice of command seemed a mixture of beast and human. Women shrieked and fled before him, and he had the satisfaction of seeing them indeed fall over the rough benches. With oaths and shouts his men followed, and many camp meeting folks were knocked down and bruised.

If it had not been for John Larkin, "the square man," the mob might have won. In the midst of all the excitement and noise he remained calm and wise. He had helped in resisting the attack in front, when, glancing to the right, he saw the monster dwarf approaching, knocking the people about with his long and powerful arms. Larkin put himself in his way, and as he got nearer said:

"Are you monkey, man, or devil, or the three combined? Whoever you are, you must reckon with me."

"I'm de man who can whip ary sneakin' braggin' preacher on dis ground. Dat's my holt," replied Turner.

With this he threw himself upon Larkin, and they were clasped in a close embrace. The monster dwarf gripped the preacher's body in his terrible arms with a strength like that of a grizzly bear, and it seemed to Larkin as though his ribs would crack and his breath leave him. But while the dwarf's arms were abnormally strong, his legs were weak, whereas Larkin's limbs were as sturdy as an oak tree. Besides, in his school days he had learned several wrestling tricks, and now he used one to throw Turner to the ground. There they continued to struggle for some time, the friends of each trying to help him. But by this time the mob in the other quarter had been subdued; and Jasper Very coming to the rescue of his colleague, the monster dwarf was conquered and several of his aids subdued and captured.

All the prisoners were sent to the county seat, and placed in jail, there to await their trial before the criminal court over which Judge LeMonde presided.

Edward T. Curnick

CHAPTER VI

UNDER THE PINE TREES

Judge William LeMonde lived about three miles from the camp ground we have described. He was the richest man in his township, his farm consisting of one thousand acres stretching from the Cumberland River back to some high hills about one mile distant. That part lying on the river was like a garden of the Lord for richness of soil. In this land Indian corn, tobacco, cabbage, and potatoes grew to perfection. Midway between the river and the high hills was a narrow ridge which ran parallel with the river. This natural backbone of land reached its greatest height on Mr. LeMonde's farm. But the highest point of all had been increased in size by artificial means. In prehistoric times a race of people living in this region had added earth to this hill until they had made an almost circular mound, which became a conspicuous object in the valley. Mr. LeMonde's father, who bought the farm many years before, called the hill "Mount Pisgah." He was a descendant of the French Huguenots. When he came from Louisiana he built a log house on this elevation. A few years before our narrative opens Mr. William LeMonde had removed this log house and built a spacious mansion of brick. It was the only brick building for miles around.

The mansion Judge LeMonde erected was an ornament to this beautiful site. It was two stories high, crowned with a French mansard roof. It faced the river and a country road which ran along the river bank. The visitor stepped upon a broad piazza, and then entered through a wide and ornamented doorway a large hall from which ascended a broad flight of stairs. On the left was a spacious drawing-room, carpeted with an imported Brussels and adorned with several oil paintings. It contained a piano, an instrument seldom seen in those days. Back of this room was the owner's study or private apartment. On the right was a room half the size of the drawing-room, all finished in white, containing on the river side a fine bay-window. This room was fitted up with much taste as a family living-room. At the rear of this was a large dining-room, and beyond this a kitchen in which the colored cook, Aunt Dinah, ruled supreme. On the second floor were several large bedchambers furnished in a neat and becoming manner. One hundred yards west of the house, on the ridge, was a cluster of negro cabins, and beyond these an immense barn, the largest in the county.

Viola LeMonde was an only daughter of Judge LeMonde. She had one brother, George, two years younger than herself. Her father and mother almost idolized her, and gave her advantages far beyond those living around her. A fine female boarding school then existed at Cincinnati, Ohio, to which she was sent, and there she remained three years, gaining that knowledge deemed best for young ladies in those days: the common branches of education and the higher accomplishments of music and drawing. At the time of which we write she was in her nineteenth year, and was known far and near for her beauty of mind and person. She was a perfect blonde. A bright light sparkled in her blue eyes; her golden hair was simply arranged over temples and brows beautifully formed. The color of her face was like a delicate peach, white with a blending of red. Her nose was of Grecian type,

Edward T. Curnick

mouth firmly chiseled and of medium size, while the cherry red lips when parted showed two rows of pearl-like teeth. Her chin was pear-shaped, and revealed decision of character. Her whole appearance gave one the impression of intelligence, purity, and benevolence. She was of medium height, and her figure would have served as a model for the skill of a Phidias. Her greatest accomplishment was music. Her voice was a high soprano, and its naturally pure tone was improved by cultivation under the best teachers.

Jasper Very's preaching appointments included the home of Judge LeMonde, and he was given a hearty welcome from the first to his house. Naturally he had seen the daughter Viola and had conversed with her several times at the mansion and at church. He soon found that she was superior to all the young ladies in the neighborhood both in strength of mind and education. To this she added a bright and deep religious experience. We must confess that the ranger's frequent visits to "Mt. Pisgah" were not wholly on church business.

On a bright afternoon appeared a select company of preachers, including Jasper Very and John Larkin, sitting under the lovely pine trees fronting Judge LeMonde's mansion.

The judge had invited them to his house to rest a day or two after the labors of the camp meeting.

The host and his beautiful daughter had joined the group of ministers.

They were a happy and merry lot as they looked over the tall, green fields of corn, and beyond to the glorious trees lining the river bank, and the sparkling stream seen between the trunks of the trees.

John Larkin was in his best mood, and the different subjects of conversation reminded him of many stories. They were talking of a sallow-cheeked preacher who was leaving his church located on Salt River.

"That makes me think of the illiterate preacher I heard of, who lived in the northern part of the State," said Larkin. "He was about to give up his church, and so delivered a farewell address thus: 'My dear bretherin-ah and sisterin-ah, I am about to leave you-ah, and I feel solemncholy-ah, I can tell you-ah. This mornin' as I was ridin' to this appintment-ah I looked up to the leaves of the trees-ah, and they seemed to be sayin', 'Good-by, Brother Crawford-ah.' And then I see the little birds singin' in the woods, and I fancied they said, 'Good-by, good-by, Brother Crawford-ah.' Then I gazed at the purty squirrels runnin' along the ground and climbin' up the trees, and they 'peared to be barkin', 'Good-bye, O good-bye, Brother Crawford-ah!' After awhile I come to a lot of pigs awallerin' in mud by the roadside. When my hoss-ah got just opposite, they got up and gave some loud grunts—whoo! whoo! whoo!—and that scart my hoss-ah, and he threw me in the dirt and ran away-ah. I ris my eyes to look at my hoss-ah, and there he was a-gallopin' down the road with his mane and tail a-flyin', and he looked back at me and seemed to be sayin', 'Good-by, Brother Crawford-ah; good-by, Brother Crawford-ah.'"

"It is a great pity," remarked Judge LeMonde, "that religion sometimes must run through such rough channels to water the soil of morality and piety when it deserves the best training of mind and voice."

"God can use very ignorant Hardshell preachers in building up his kingdom if their own hearts are right before him," said Jasper Very; "but if they are imposters, they are a disgrace and injury to the sacred calling.

"I met a fellow once across the Ohio River whose name was Sargent. He assumed the name of Halycon Church, and proclaimed himself the millennial messenger. He professed to see visions, fall into trances, and to converse with angels. We had a camp meeting near Marietta, and this fellow came to it. He wanted to preach, and upon being refused pretended to swoon away. One night he lit a cigar and got some powder, and walked away about one hundred yards where stood a large stump. He put the powder on the stump and touched it with his cigar. The flash was seen by many in the camp, and they came up to find Sargent lying on the ground. After a long time he came to, and told the people he had a message from God for them. Seeing so many there, I lit a lantern and went down to investigate. Stepping up to the stump, I smelled the sulphur and saw the mark of the burnt powder, and near the stump lay the cigar. As he was talking to the people, I stepped up to him and asked him if an angel had appeared to him in a flash of light. He said, 'Yes.' 'Sargent,' said I, 'did not that angel smell of brimstone?' 'Why,' said he 'do you ask such a foolish question?' 'Because,' said I, 'if an angel has spoken to you, he was from the lake which burneth with fire and brimstone;' and, raising my voice, I said, 'I smell sulphur now.' I walked to the stump and showed the people his wicked trick. They were very indignant and called him a vile imposter, and soon he left, and we were no more troubled with him and his brimstone angels."

"What a shame that men will take the livery of heaven in which to serve the evil one," said Viola LeMonde. "Hypocrisy is like a counterfeit coin: it is not only worthless in itself, but it also makes men suspect the genuine money."

"Poor Richard says, 'Honesty is the best policy,' and that holds good in preaching as in other things," remarked Larkin.

Jasper Very added: "Men who are dishonest cheat themselves. They narrow their souls. They grasp after a substance
and find a shadow. A sure Nemesis follows the present gain.
The great poet says: 'Who steals my purse steals trash.'"

"Sam Wiles is a case in point," said Judge LeMonde. "He
surely is cheating himself. But what gave him the disposition
he possesses? Heredity and environment; and not one man in
a thousand will rise out of these. The fellow has some good
in him; but it is strangled by his bent and surroundings, like
good seed choked by thorns. What say you, Mr. Larkin?"

"There is only one hope for him, that is religion, which he
seems to despise and reject. His superior gifts, making him a
leader of the moonshine gang, constitute him a greater
menace to law-abiding people. The Bengal tiger kills more
prey than the common wild-cat which sometimes roams
these surrounding woods. I am told that Wiles is the ring
leader in many reckless acts, and will stop at nothing to gain
his ends. Zibe Turner, called the monster dwarf, is his right-
hand man, who will pick his chestnuts from the fire, though
he burn his impish fingers in so doing."

"You remember, papa," said Viola, "when we and a few
friends had that picnic two weeks ago on 'Silver Knob' we
passed by the cabin where Sam Wiles lives? I felt sad to see
his poor mother in her faded and torn calico dress in the little
front yard. She was stirring some food in an iron kettle
which was over a fire of logs. Her eyes had such a dull,
discouraged look in them. The children were dirty and half
dressed, and how the dogs barked as we came near! The lot
of the 'poor whites' in Kentucky is indeed unfortunate. Even
the slaves look down upon them.

"When I saw the Wiles family and other families like them in
their low condition I said in my heart: 'Cannot something be

done for the comfort and uplift of these people?' Gentlemen, I put the question to you this afternoon."

After a silence of some duration Jasper Very spoke:

"I am sure something ought to be done and can be done to brighten the lives of these poor folks. They live in the hills remote from church and Sunday School, which they never attend, and exist as heathen in a Christian country. Their forefathers in England were among the best yeomen of the land, and I believe many of these have the making of good, honest, upright citizens."

"I think it is possible to organize a community school—a combination of Sunday School and day school—for these dwellers in the hills," added John Larkin. "As I was riding down 'Sinex Knob' the other day I passed a settler's cabin, larger and better built than most dwellings in that section. The owner's name is Mart Spink. He has a wife and several bright-looking children. Perhaps he would grant the use of his living-room for school purposes. The Wiles family and a number of other families live near enough to attend."

"My thought coincides with the suggestion of Mr. Larkin," said Viola LeMonde. "We ought to have such a school. In it we should teach the truths of religion and also the common branches of learning. Moreover, we should help the whole community—the farmers to better cultivate their lands and their minds; the farmers' wives to improve their house-keeping, to get out of the ruts, and to take a wider interest in developing their own intellects and those of their children; the sons to have noble ambitions in life and to prepare to achieve them; the daughters, besides the moral and intellec-tual training they receive, to learn sewing, knitting, cooking, and other forms of domestic science. Yes, and I would have a primitive dispensary, that the neighbors might have at least first aid in case of sickness or accident. Tomorrow I will have my servant Mose Williams to drive me in the phaeton to David Hester's house. There I will talk with his daughter Henrietta, and I am sure I can induce her to join me in the project. Together we will explore the ground and make a beginning.

"I shall ask you gentlemen to aid us in every way in your power by sympathy, advice, prayer, and work."

"Most gladly will I do so on one condition," Very responded with a laugh, "that is, that we now adjourn to the parlor, and you will favor us with music both instrumental and vocal."

"Would you have me to be so selfish as to be the whole show?" rejoined Viola. "I will do nothing of the kind, sir; but I will play and sing if the company will unite with me in singing the hymns."

This demand was heartily accepted, and the group at once left the shade of the pine trees for the parlor.

Christianity is said to be the only religion that can be sung. It began with the angels' song, and its music will continue on earth till it is transferred to the song of redemption in heaven.

The hymns of Christendom are among its most cherished and valuable possessions. They sound the depths of the human heart. They express the varied emotions of the soul.

It is no wonder that Jasper Very requested Viola LeMonde to play and sing.

We behold this queen of song seated at the piano, while around her stood her father and her mother (the mother having just come in) and the preachers.

First Viola favored them with several instrumental selections from the great masters. It was interesting to watch her hands. They were perfect in size, shape and color. The slender fingers were tipped with nails curved like almonds. They struck the keys with a precision, force and grace, leaving nothing to be desired. The quick interplay of mind and muscle interpreted the music to her hearers in a way almost to produce tears.

After a rest during which some bright, witty remarks, like sparks, passed from one to another, they prepared to sing some of the great hymns of the church. They were well equipped for their task. Viola's voice was pure, sweet, soulful, and high. She might have been a sister of Jenny Lind. Her mother sang also in a rich and expressive manner. Jasper Very possessed a fine deep bass voice. John Larkin sang an acceptable tenor. All the rest were able to use their voices in song.

As by common understanding they began with songs of adoration and praise. Each one entered into the spirit of that inspiring hymn of Charles Wesley:

> "O for a thousand tongues to sing
> My great Redeemer's praise,
> The glories of my God and King,
> The triumphs of his grace."

The persons here were advanced agents in bringing civilization to Kentucky. They had the heroic spirit. These preachers had endured hardness as good soldiers of Jesus Christ. They had climbed mountains, crossed valleys, forded streams, slept in the open, encountered wild beasts and base and desperate men. Songs to cheer, encourage, and strengthen their faith and zeal were needed and provided. Naturally they desired to sing on this occasion. So the company sang with zest Luther's great battle hymn:

"A mighty fortress is our God,
A bulwark never failing:
Our helper he, amid the flood
Of mortal ills prevailing."

Then was sung that hymn of triumphant trust, beginning:

"Though troubles assail, and dangers affright,
Though friends should all fail, and foes all unite,
Yet one thing secures us, whatever betide,
The promise assures us, The Lord will provide."

The pioneers of that day had an exultant experience of the religion they professed and taught. Viola next turned to hymns expressing this state. She and those gathered around her sang them with joyous, even ecstatic, acclamation:

"O happy day, that fixed my choice
On thee, my Savior and my God!
Well may this glowing heart rejoice,
And tell its rapture all abroad."

And:

"Love divine, all love excelling,
Joy of heaven, to earth come down;
Fix in us thy humble dwelling,
All thy faithful mercies crown."

After they had sung a number of other hymns, Jasper Very said to Viola LeMonde: "I have heard, Miss LeMonde, that you have composed the music to a new paraphrase of the Ninety-First Psalm. I am sure we should all be delighted to hear you sing your music to the words. Will you kindly favor us by so doing?"

Viola LeMonde replied: "I am not an adept at composing music, but the words of this poem impressed me, and I joined them to an air which came to me almost sponta- neously. I shall take pleasure in singing this melody, if you will be charitable in criticism." Thus speaking she sang the following words simply but with much feeling:

The Saint's Refuge.

Dwelling in God's secret place,
Safe doth his beloved lie,
Shaded by his sovereign grace
From the tempests fierce and high.
Love Divine will hear his prayer,
Be his refuge and defense;
Save him from the fowler's snare,
And the noisome pestilence.
Sheltered 'neath the Father's wings,
Covered with his pinions wide,
Truth the ransomed homeward brings,
Shielding him on every side.

Fear recedes from terror's night,
Harmless flies the dart by day;
In the darkness or the light
Wasting death shall flee away.
Sees he, falling in their pride,
Twice five thousand wicked men;
But destruction's wrathful tide
Shall not touch his garments then.
Angels, ministrant, shall fly
From their dazzling upper zones,
Charged by heaven's Majesty
Him to keep from crushing stones.

On the lion, bold and dread,
Seeking ever to devour,
And the hissing serpent's head,
He shall tread with victor's pow'r.
God will wipe away his tears;
Grant him honor and release;
Crown his life with length of years;
Save, and keep in perfect peace.

Edward T. Curnick

CHAPTER VII

THE HORSE RACE

We left Sam Wiles, Zibe Turner and other disturbers of the peace in the county jail. In due time they were brought before Judge LeMonde for trial. They were found guilty and sentenced to prison for one month.

A few days after their liberation the following conversation took place:

Turner: "Most all de folks on de hills and in de valleys air goin' to de races tomorrer, and I look for a gay o' time."

Wiles: "Yes, and all de niggers that can get off'n work will be there too."

Turner: "Dat feller from Lexington has a right smart of a hoss. You know he wants me to ride him in de last race, and I'm bound to beat George LeMonde, if beat is in de critter. His hoss stands seventeen hands high, is rangy in de legs, has a deep chest, and has a will to go. He can easily bear my weight, and you know dat dey count me de best jockey in de whul county. If I can't win by far (fair) means, I will by foul."

Wiles: "I hearn dat Jack Ketcham's sorrel goes like de wind, and Jack's hoss is goin' to be in de big race."

Turner: "George LeMonde has been speeding his bay over de track for days, and he will get every bit of go out of him. His mother and sister are dead set agin hoss-racin' and dey are begging him not to ride; but George likes de sport too well to please dem."

Wiles: "Mr. Rawlins, of Lexington, swears by his black, and will put up a great deal of money. George will try to match it, and ol' farmer Ketcham won't be slow with his cash."

Turner: "It will be an excitin' time, and I low, as many will see de races as went to de big camp meetin'."

Wiles: "Well, Zibe, you must stick to your hoss like a monkey, and do your best to win de money and down that upstart, George LeMonde."

With this remark the two men separated.

George LeMonde was a youth about seventeen years of age, well-built, good-looking, full of life and vigor, and at this time engaged in that serious occupation, common to many young men, sowing his wild oats. He was boisterous and rather reckless, but not vicious. His moral nature was touched by evil, but not yet corrupted. However, he had begun to walk in the broad way of youthful folly, and was in great danger of going its full length. He was restrained from drinking the full cup of unlawful indulgence more by the prayers, example, and love of his mother and sister than by the correct moral life of his father.

The greatest danger to that priceless thing, character, which

Edward T. Curnick

confronted him was his association with the hillside young men. They never felt that he was one in desire and purpose with them; but sometimes he would meet them on the big road by Franklin Schoolhouse or occasionally go to their cabins on the hills. Then he would sip lightly their moonshine whiskey, join in their coarse talk, and share in their few pastimes.

George LeMonde probably inherited his love for horses. His father, Judge LeMonde, for many years had raised his own colts from the best stock he could procure. On his broad acres they had every chance to develop their physical powers. His fields produced an abundance of the best corn and hay. Skirting the hill which bounded his farm on the north were extensive meadows rich with grass. Here his blooded stock browsed, ran and grew. It was under similar conditions that many Kentucky horses were raised early in the nineteenth century, becoming sires of the greatest racing stock in the world.

At the time of which we write Judge LeMonde owned a bay, of his own raising, which was his pride and joy. The horse, Velox by name, was far and away better than any other he had ever possessed. He was known throughout the entire county as a splendid specimen of horseflesh, and for beauty and utility had won the blue ribbon at a number of surrounding fairs.

When George LeMonde reached his sixteenth birthday his father gave him this fine animal. The son was delighted with the gift, and took the best care of Velox, often feeding him with his own hand. George rode his horse so much that he learned all the traits and peculiarities of his steed; for horses, like men, have their own individual make-up and notions. On the other hand, Velox got to know, trust, love and obey his master. He would come at his call, and could be guided when on a journey nearly as well by the motions of his owner's body as by the rein.

George LeMonde decided to enter Velox for the race which was soon to take place, and many times did he ride his willing steed over the race course to prepare for the great event.

Horse racing then, as now, was one of the most popular diversions of multitudes in Kentucky, but the preparations then were quite primitive. The track was laid in a level piece of ground some miles from Judge LeMonde's farm. It was in the form of a circle, and was one mile in circumference. The inclosure was protected by a rough fence, hewn out of logs. Within the course, near the starting place, and on the inside of the track, was a stand upon which the judges of the races sat. Some rough seats were provided for a part of the spectators, but most of the people stood during the races.

Saturday dawned clear and beautiful. It was a perfect day to bring out the speed of the racers. The time selected was near the last of August, and a crispness in the air gave a faint indication of coming autumn. People from far and wide had come to enjoy the sport. They made the occasion a holiday. Many came on horseback and by team, and families brought well-filled baskets of fried chicken, corn pone, blackberry pie, and other good things to refresh the inner man.

A number of minor races were run by horses in harness and under the saddle, which only increased the people's appetite for the grand event of the day. At four in the afternoon the three horses were called for the two-mile race. Their riders soon brought them from their stalls to a position in front of the grand stand and judges. The steeds were all in perfect condition, their glossy coats shining with bright luster in the afternoon sun. The horses seemed to feel the meaning of the

Edward T. Curnick

occasion. They champed their bits and moved about restlessly as though impatient to be off. Their riders, however, had them under good control, and now the judges tossed the coin for choice of position on the track. Zibe Turner secured the inside place, George LeMonde came next, and Hiram Ketcham, Farmer Ketcham's son of eighteen, was on the outer rim of the circle, next to the fence.

The grand stand, composed of rough boards, was filled with the best dressed citizens of the county: while far down the track, and separated from it by a frail line of fence, stood a great company of tall Kentucky pioneers with their wives and children. Many negroes were also in the crowd, interested spectators, and the small boy was much in evidence.

A silence fell upon the waiting throng as the three horses, bearing their riders, proceeded up the track a few rods to make a dash for the line. The signal was given, and they came like three thunderbolts to the starting place; but reaching this they were not abreast, and another start must be made. They tried four times before they got away in line, when some one shouted: "Now they are off!" For a few paces they were neck and neck; but then Hiram Ketcham's sorrel, though on the outer circle forged ahead. When the half-mile point was reached, the sorrel was several lengths in the lead, and Zibe Turner's black was leading George LeMonde's bay by a dozen feet. They came in this position down the home stretch, and as they crossed the line a great cheering rose from the crowd. Turner's friends from the hills were there in large numbers, and were the loudest in their shouts. "Go it, Zibe; you'll beat, old boy!" "Hurrah for de black! push him along!" "I'll bet my money on de Lexington hoss!" were some of the words that were shouted at Turner as he dashed past the starting point for the second mile. Hiram Ketcham did not lack for admirers, who encouraged him with cheers and waving of hats and handkerchiefs.

Many of the farmers living in the rich river bottom seemed to be partial to the sorrel horse. George LeMonde's friends were plentiful in the grand stand and, in fact, throughout the crowd. They were somewhat disappointed to behold him the last in the race; but they saw that Velox was going well, and they had hopes for his winning during the next mile.

As for young LeMonde, he saw nothing and gave heed to nothing except the business in hand. Only once did he raise his eyes from looking straight ahead between the ears of his noble horse, and that was when he was passing the grandstand. Then he gave a swift look in that direction, and was repaid by seeing a young girl of some sixteen years of age, Stella Nebeker by name, dressed in a pure white muslin gown with short sleeves, waving a delicate handkerchief toward him. For an instant their eyes met, then he looked along the race course as before.

LeMonde had a method in his racing which he was now working. He knew the reserved powers which were in his horse, and he purposely held him back from putting forth his greatest speed at the beginning. Turner, the monster dwarf, was also using all his skill in horse racing. His monkeyish face was lighted up with a look of more intelligence than usual, which made his ugly features more forbidding and repulsive. His eyes shone with excitement, determination, and reckless courage. His teeth were clenched, and the muscles of his lips drawn over them gave him an expression half laughing, half demoniac. On the first round his cap had fallen off, and the shaggy hair of his head and face streamed in the wind, adding greatly to the fierceness of his looks. He had perfect control of himself and horse, and rode like a centaur, ready to take any advantage which circumstances or guile threw in his way. He also had held in his horse with bit and bridle, reserving his best efforts for the closing part of the race.

Edward T. Curnick

During the first half of the second mile Turner knew that it was necessary for him to lessen the distance between himself and Hiram Ketcham, and LeMonde realized that he must soon close the gap separating Turner and himself. Almost at the same time they gave their horses more rein, and they sprang to their work with increased speed. Ketcham had taken advantage of his lead by crossing the track and taking the narrow arc of the circle. The three horses were trotting in a line, all hugging the inside track. Very soon the distance between the sorrel and the black was diminished, and before the half mile point was reached the monster dwarf turned his horse toward the center of the track to pass Ketcham. Just beyond the half-mile point Turner's black passed Ketcham's sorrel, and LeMonde's bay was neck and neck with the black. A few rods more, and it was plain to be seen that the bay was forging ahead of the black.

The monster dwarf saw at once the advantage of his rival, and hissing through his teeth in a low voice the words: "Dat's my holt," brought his short cowhide whip down with force upon the withers of Velox. It was the act of a jockey utterly without principle, an act execrated by every true Kentucky sportsman.

The splendid animal never before had felt the lash of a whip. The blow had the effect desired by the dwarf. It broke the gait of the bay horse. The stroke was so unexpected and painful that the horse gave a bound forward and upward that almost unseated the rider. Then he plunged along the track with irregular strides, sometimes rushing to the sides and then to the center.

Though taken by surprise George LeMonde acted with decision and judgment. He held his mount with a firm hand, and added to the strength of his arm the soothing effect of his voice: "Steady, steady, Velox! Your master did not strike you. He loves you. Steady, steady, good horse! Velox! Velox! Velox!" By these means young LeMonde renewed the race, though the other horses were a considerable distance in advance.

In the meantime a large number of the spectators had seen the despicable act and roared their disapproval. Some shook their fists at the monster dwarf, and cried for speedy punishment for his vile trick. This outburst of indignation made him fear again to molest the bay horse.

Now George knew that the time had come for Velox to use his utmost powers. He knew that the horse had great reserved fountains of strength in him, and believed he could still win the race. As for the horse, he seemed alive to the situation. Perhaps he felt a proud resentment at the insult and injury put upon him. His eyes flashed fire. His nostrils were dilated until the red blood showed through his veins. Man and horse gave to each other courage and confidence; they appeared no longer to be two creatures, but had been merged into a single unit of astonishing force and capacity. LeMonde's whole soul was absorbed with one thought—to pass the other horses and to cross the line first. He leaned farther front in the saddle, lowering his head to reduce the resistance of the air. His face almost touched the flying mane of his horse.

Again he spoke to his mount: "Steady, my Velox boy; we are nearing the end. It will soon be over; but you must pass these horses, and win the race." With this remark LeMonde gave free rein to his horse, pressed his knees a little tighter against the animal's sides, and gave him a light touch with the whip. The noble horse instantly responded to his master's urge. He released fold after fold of knotted muscle, his stride increased, and when his hoofs descended, they seemed to spurn the ground. Now as steady as a Corliss engine this ultimate unit of the animal and mechanical world rushed on,

Edward T. Curnick

and was seen to be gaining on the other horses.

At a quarter of a mile from the home stake the sorrel horse was passed, but still the result seemed uncertain. Then young LeMonde appeared as a Jehu incarnate. He pressed the horse's flanks with his heels and shouted into the very ears of his mount: "Velox, we must win, we will win, we are going to win." With this remark, for the first time in his life he brought the whip down hard upon the glossy hide of his steed. The animal increased his speed, and went thundering down the home stretch after the black. It is a case of blood against time and space. The bay gains! He has closed the distance between them! His head is on a line with the other's shoulder! They are only one hundred yards from the goal! The grand stand is wild with shouting! Those standing near the track, unconscious of what they do, are throwing hats, handkerchiefs and umbrellas into the air, and yelling like mad men! The judges are sighting the line! They see a horse's brown head and shoulders pass the line, then a black head appears, and Velox has won by a neck's length.

CHAPTER VIII

PRAYER IN A DANCE HALL

When the three horses crossed the finishing line, covered with sweat and foam, LeMonde and Ketcham soon brought their mounts to a stop. Not so the monster dwarf. Fearing that the crowd might do him personal injury he rode the black horse directly to the stable. He was almost beside himself with rage and disappointment. He ground his teeth together, and froth showed upon his lips. His face was hideous in expression. He shook his fist in the direction of the race course, and cursed the victorious horse and rider with terrible oaths.

To Sam Wiles, who had come up, he said: "Anudder chance will come. I'll git even wid dat proud aristocrat yit. I'm goin' to git back all de money I lost today, and mo' too."

A different scene was taking place near the grand stand. When George LeMonde, with flushed face and bright eyes, dismounted from his horse, he was at once surrounded by an admiring crowd who showered him with congratulations. They praised his skill as a horseman, his coolness in a time of danger and emergency, and his good nature under great provocation. Many were the admirers of Velox. They patted his shoulders, stroked his head and commented on his beauty of color and form. The horse took it in good part, and seemed to consider it a proper tribute to the steed who won the race.

Among the rest who shook George heartily by the hand was a stout, broad-featured man of about forty, who was dressed in a good suit of blue jeans and wore what was uncommon in those days, a large diamond pin in his shirt front. His name was Costello Nebeker, and he was a tavern keeper on a country road not many miles away. The girl with a white dress and shapely arm whom George saw as he flashed past the grand stand was Stella Nebeker, the sixteen-year-old daughter of this tavern keeper. She came forward, and in a happy way congratulated him upon his success. They had known each other for some time; for we are sorry to say, George on various occasions, having been at the tavern with some of his young friend, had indulged in the liquors which Nebeker kept for sale. While at this tavern George had become acquainted with Stella Nebeker, and she soon found a place in his affections. She was comely, vivacious and sensible, fond of society, a natural leader among her set, having most of the accomplishments furnished by the schools and social gatherings of their neighborhood.

Nebeker said to George in his loud and hearty way: "LeMonde, today you have covered yourself and horse with glory, and incidentally have put a good many dollars into my jeans pocket. Now you and your friends must celebrate this victory by a layout (feast) and dance at my house. Next Saturday will be moonlight, and Stella and I will invite our friends and you must ask yours to come, and we will have a jolly supper, and wash it down with some first-class Kentucky whisky, and wind up the meeting with a party dance."

George agreed to this proposal; and after bidding the tavern keeper and his lovely daughter a kind adieu, he departed to the stable, whither his faithful servant, Mose, had led his horse.

Costello Nebeker lived about ten miles from Mr. LeMonde's plantation in rather a rough and hilly country. For a number of years he had kept a public house; and as his place was the only one of this kind for many miles around, and as it fronted on a much-traveled county road, he had many customers at his bar and guests in his tavern. His house was a large frame structure, the lower part of which was used for a bar and lounging place and the rear for a dance hall. On the second floor were several sleeping rooms, some of which were occupied by the keeper and his family, and the rest were prepared for travelers.

The sky was clear and the woods beautiful on the following Saturday evening. As the sun began to hide his brilliant rays behind the noble hills covered with regal forests, and the moon, nearing its full, was already throwing a silvery light over the scene, those invited to the supper and dance were making their way, some in buggies along the main road, but most on horseback, coming down hills and across valleys, all moving to a central point, the tavern house.

It is not our design to dwell upon that feast, which consisted of most of the good things then in season in Kentucky, but to come at once to the dance and to a striking incident which occurred there.

Rather late in the evening, after dancing had been going on for some time, Jasper Very rode up to the tavern. He had been on a long preaching tour, and was tired and hungry. When he had dismounted, he asked the proprietor if he could lodge there for the night. Mr. Nebeker politely told him he could stay, but he was afraid he would not enjoy himself

Edward T. Curnick

very well, as a dance was in progress. Jasper then inquired how far it was to a suitable house where he could put up for the night, and was told seven miles. He felt in his present condition that this was too far, and said that if the tavern keeper would treat him civilly and feed his horse well by his leave he would stay. This was promised him, and Very dismounted and went in. He quietly took a seat in one corner of the room, and the dancing continued. While musing upon many things and wishing in his heart he could do those people good, and having finally made up his mind to ask the privilege of preaching there the next day, he was surprised to see a beautiful and ruddy young lady, who was no other than Stella Nebeker, walk gracefully up to him, drop a handsome courtesy, and pleasantly, with a winning smile, invite him to dance with her. Jasper Very in his life had been in many strange situations, but this was an experience unlike any he had hitherto passed through. He could hardly understand his thoughts or feelings, but in a moment he resolved on a desperate experiment. He arose as gracefully as he could, with many emotions crowding upon his mind. Stella with much grace moved to his right side. Jasper grasped her right hand with his left hand, while she leaned her left arm on his right arm. In this position they walked on the floor.

The whole company seemed pleased at this act of politeness in a young lady shown to a stranger. The colored musician began to put his fiddle in the best order. Jasper here asked the fiddler to hold a minute, and, addressing the company, said: "Friends, for several years I have not undertaken any matter of importance without first asking the blessing of God upon it, and I desire now to ask God's blessing upon this beautiful young lady, who has shown such an act of politeness to a total stranger, and upon the whole company."

Here he grasped the young lady's hand tightly and said: "Let us all kneel down and pray." With this he dropped upon his knees, and began praying with all the power he possessed. Stella tried to get loose from him, but he held her tightly.

This unexpected act threw the whole company into excitement and disorder. Stella seized by an emotion which she could not control, fell upon her knees. Some of the dancers kneeled, some stood, some sat still with curious looks upon their faces, while others fled as in terror. The fiddler ran off into the kitchen saying: "Lord a marcy, what de matter. What's dat mean? Prayin' in a dance hall! Dis beats anyting dis niggar ever saw."

Jasper Very continued to pray with loud voice and great unction. Some soon began weeping softly, others cried out aloud in their deep feeling, and some asked God for mercy. After a while Jasper arose from his knees and commenced an exhortation, after which he sang a hymn.

Stella Nebeker was so affected by the service and by the deep convictions of her heart that she remained for a long time prostrate on the floor, crying earnestly for pardon. This strange meeting continued nearly all night; and when it was ended, fifteen of those dancers had obtained pardon for their sins. Stella was one of them, George LeMonde was another and the tavern keeper was a third. From this dance room a great revival spread throughout that part of the country.

Edward T. Curnick

CHAPTER IX

WANTED, A MISSION SCHOOL

Let us follow Miss Viola LeMonde and Miss Henrietta Harvey in their effort to organize a Sunday School among the "Poor Whites."

It was a beautiful day in September when the two young ladies seated in the phaeton drawn by Velox and Dolly and driven by faithful Mose made their way into the hill country. Their object was to visit as many families in a remote section as possible, and try to get their consent to join the proposed school.

After riding a number of miles they came to the family of Mart Spink. The two-room cabin in which they lived had the distinction of being built of hewn logs. It also had a "lean-to," or low ell, attached to the larger part.

Fortunately they found the "old man," Mart Spink, at home. He seemed surprised to behold such a fine turnout stop at his door, but showed a native gallantry as he came to the carriage.

"Howdy, ladies, I'se glad to see you. Won't you 'light, and walk into de house?"

"Thank you," replied Viola. "My name is Viola LeMonde, and this is my friend, Miss Henrietta Harvey. We have come to consult you on some important business, and shall be glad to step into your cottage."

With this remark they both dismounted from the phaeton, and passed into the house.

Here they found the whole family, and Mr. Spink introduced them in order to the ladies—his wife, Lucinda, his oldest daughter, Susanna, then Elmira, Robert and Jonathan.

Mart Spink invited the ladies to be seated, and they sat down on splint-bottom chairs.

Viola LeMonde opened the business in hand: "Mr. Spink, some of us living in the bottoms, knowing that you dwell so far away from any church that you and your neighbors cannot well attend public religious services, have decided to start a Sunday School in this locality, if we can find a suitable place, and if the people are willing to come to it.

"Not long ago Rev. John Larkin, whom perhaps you have seen, suggested your house as the best place in these hills in which to begin a school. What do you say to the proposition?"

Mart Spink replied: "Well, I was born in Nashville, Tennessee, and lived thar with my parents till I was eight years old. I went to school thar and learned how to read and write a little. I also went to church and Sunday School some."

Then they took up land here in de backwoods, and since that time I have had mighty little chance to larn out of books and to go to meetin'.

"Yes, I would be rale glad to have you start a school in my house, if Lucinda is willin'. What do you say, wife?"

Lucinda: "Let us have de school by all means; de sooner de better. I want it for your sake, Mart, and mine, but specially for our boys and girls."

So the consent was given and the matter settled.

Susanna Spink, the oldest child, sat opposite Viola LeMonde during the conversation. She was fourteen years old, and was of such striking beauty that both the visitors were impressed by it. Her chief attraction was her eyes. Once seen they could never be forgotten. The eyebrows were dark and of medium size. The lashes were black and long. Her eyes were large, clear, deep blue in color. One could look down into their wondrous depths and imagine one could see the very soul of the child.

Susanna was all attention during the talk about the school. She spoke no word, but the look of her eyes spoke volumes to Viola. She knew that the child was intensely interested in the project. That hour by an invisible and mysterious power the souls of the woman and child were welded together into a union of friendship and devotion which death itself could not part. Neither suspected at this time what a test of this devotion was to appear in the future.

Highly pleased with the success of their first visit the ladies entered the carriage, and Viola directed Mose to drive to the home of the Wiles family. Arriving there they were greeted by the furious barking of a pack of dogs and by the staring looks of some of the children. Mrs. Wiles was in the front yard hanging out some faded and frayed clothing on the line.

We must give the names of this interesting family. Those at

home were Mrs. Deborah Wiles and her children Ephraim, Priscilla, Martha, and Ruth. The father, Simon, was absent, and also his precious son, Sam, whose acquaintance we have already made. The remaining son, Reuben, was visiting a near neighbor about three miles distant. However much of original depravity existed in this family the parents were determined that they should be fortified with biblical names.

Mrs. Wiles showed small courtesy to the strangers, for she did not call off the dogs or speak to the visitors till she had hung out to dry the last remaining piece of washing.

Then she turned to the carriage, and inquired of the ladies what they wanted. Viola and Henrietta without any invitation stepped down from the vehicle, and made known their mission.

Mrs. Wiles expressed herself unfavorable to the idea. She said they were gittin' along well enough without any church meetin's, and they did not want any of de high-toned people from de bottoms to come up there, putting on airs, treating them as ignorant, and no 'count white trash, and making fun of their farms and houses.

But different words sprang from the lips of Ephraim and Priscilla.

Ephraim, the boy who a few years before had discovered Wind Cave, now grown to a good sized youth, said: "You are wrong, ma. Most of us around here are a low down set without books or religion. If these ladies are willin' to spend their time to come all this way and teach us larnin' and de Bible, I say we ought to thank them, and help them to start de school."

Priscilla said she agreed with her brother and thought it was

Edward T. Curnick

time they "were gittin' out of their pore way of livin'," and she would be glad "to jine de school" if her mother would let her.

Mrs. Wiles gave a cold consent, and the carriage drove away, the ladies thankful that they had secured at least two more advocates of their scheme.

Mose spoke to his mettled steeds and soon they were drawing the carriage over an unfrequented road through a deep forest to the cabin of Harrop Sneath. He and his house were typical of the poorest of the "poor whites." His cabin consisted of one room, about fourteen feet square, with one door and no windows. It was made of unhewn logs plastered with clay. The only daylight which entered the cabin came through the door when open and down the chimney. On the inside stood a bedstead made of poles stuck between the logs of the angle, the outside corner supported by a crotched stick. The table was a huge hewn log, standing on four pegs. A log bench or two took the place of chairs. The cooking utensils consisted of an iron pot, which hung in the big chimney, a kettle and skillet and a few pewter and tin dishes. The loft was the sleeping place of most of the children. It was reached by a ladder of wooden pins driven into the logs.

Harrop Sneath was too lazy and shiftless to work much. He cultivated in a careless way a small piece of cleared ground around his cabin on which he raised a little Indian corn. The meat for his family was provided by his rifle, for the woods abounded in game—deer, wild turkeys, etc.

It was in such a cabin that Abraham Lincoln was born in another part of Kentucky about this time.

When Viola and Henrietta entered the clearing Sneath was sitting in the sun on a log bench in front of his cabin. He was a man in middle life and like most of the hillside settlers was the father of several children.

The young ladies addressed him pleasantly, and asked after his family and his crops.

He replied, that "de old woman and de kids war right peart; that de crops were most a dead failure because of de dry spell." He "'lowed a dry spell war mighty bad for crops on hillside farms." In this he was quite right.

By this time the "old woman" and some of the kids had come into the yard. Among them was Jemima Sneath, the oldest daughter. She was apparently about twenty years of age, and was a large, healthy young woman.

Henrietta Harvey was the speaker this time, and in a clear and emphatic manner made their mission known. She told them about the school, what a blessing it would be to the community, the families and each one. It would improve their minds, help to remove the evils which all knew existed in the hills, help to put the farmers on their feet by showing them how to raise better crops.

Trying to awaken a greater interest in the father she said: "Mr. Sneath, when you are not working on your place or hunting, how do you pass the time?"

He answered with a slow drawl: "Well, most ginerally I sot on de bench in shade in summer and in de sun in winter. Sometimes I sot and think, and sometimes I jest sot."

Such a man they felt it difficult to arouse, but when Viola added her invitations and arguments to those of her friend, poor Sneath awoke enough to the situation to hold his head up higher and widen his shoulders a trifle.

Edward T. Curnick

The one most interested was Jemima, the oldest daughter. She promised to attend the first meeting and to become a member of the school.

Viola now directed Mose to drive them still farther through the woods to the home of Zibe Turner, the monster dwarf. They would not have dared to beard this lion in his den, but knowing he had left the county for the time being, they wished, if possible, to interest his mother and sister in the school.

As they drew up to the house the dwarf's mother stood in the doorway, her daughter looking over her shoulder. The mother might have been a twin sister of Sycorax, the dam of Caliban. She was tall and slim, dressed in a coarse, hand-woven dress. Her long, scant hair fell down over her shoulders. Her face was that of a hag. Her few teeth were stained yellow with tobacco.

As soon as Viola spoke of the school, this vixen, raising her right arm to its greatest height and clenching her hand, broke out in wild vituperation:

"What do de like of ye, comin' into our hills in yer fine carriage to see how pore we air and to look down on us? Woud you uns larn us to be good in yer school? We uns air as good as you uns even if we don't live in big houses and drive fast hosses. Away with you! Me and mine will have nuthin' to do with yer mission."

In a similar vein she continued to pour out a volley of loud and abusive words, interlarding them with such oaths and curses as would have surprised a Billinsgate fishwoman.

Viola tried for a brief time to reason with her, and present their plea for the mission school, but, finding it was useless to remain longer, told Mose to drive away. When they had reached the shelter of the woods the slave said: "Ah neber hurd a deck han' on de ribber cuss and swear lak dat po' white woman."

Still these noble ladies, inspired with a high resolve to help the lowly, undismayed continued their work. In the course of two or three days a sufficient number of persons had agreed to attend the school to warrant its being opened with much promise.

CHAPTER X

THE MISSION SCHOOL ESTABLISHED

The time set for beginning the mission school was the first Sunday in October. The place, Mart Spink's sitting-room.

Mr. Spink had added to the seating capacity of his cabin by taking some long slabs and with an auger drilling holes in their round sides. Into these holes he drove wooden pegs, and thus provided serviceable benches without backs. These together with his other benches and his chairs gave sufficient seating accommodation for those who came.

It was a motley but interesting crowd that assembled in the sitting-room at two o'clock that Sunday afternoon. Of course the Spinks were there, and some members of the Wiles and Sneath families were present, and others from different homes in that section. Fourteen girls, ten boys and a few adults had come to the meeting. Besides these there were the preacher, John Larkin, Viola and George LeMonde, Henrietta Harvey, and Stella Nebeker in attendance. Jasper Very wished much to be present, but a preaching engagement kept him away.

The children were dressed somewhat better than on week days but at that their clothing was nothing to boast of. The girls were shy and ill at ease, the boys half shy and half bold.

John Larkin called the school to order, and made a few remarks.

"Dear friends, we are met here today to worship God and to study his Holy Word. I am sure you want me in your behalf to thank the ladies who visited your homes and invited you to help in starting this school, and to thank Mr. Spink and family who have so kindly opened their house for our meetings. Miss Viola LeMonde has had some hymn books placed on the benches, and she will lead us in song."

Viola knew that most of those present were not acquainted with a single religious hymn, but she thought the older ones might be able to sing some of the old favorites of the church. So she led them in singing:

"Rock of Ages, cleft for me," and "All hail the power of Jesus' name."

Those who had come to help in the school carried the tunes along very well, and Viola was surprised and pleased to hear some of the farmers and their wives join in singing these sweet songs of Zion.

Then Viola sang as a solo a beautiful and appropriate "Children's Hymn," containing these words.

"Hosanna! be the children's song,
To Christ, the children's King;
His praise, to whom our souls belong,
Let all the children sing.
Hosanna! sound from hill to hill,
And spread from plain to plain,
While louder, sweeter, clearer still,

Woods echo to the strain."

Then John Larkin said: "Let us pray." He closed his eyes, and began an earnest supplication at the throne of grace. But it might have been better for him and the school, if he had kept his eyes open while he offered his petition, and thus obeyed the Bible command: "Watch and pray." When he closed his eyes the little imps in divers parts of the room saw their chance for mischief, and were quick to embrace it.

A Sneath boy put his straw hat on the head of a boy next him, and then knocked it off with no gentle blow. This angered the other youngster and he hit back with his clenched fist. So they had it back and forth, to the amusement of all the chaps around them. Another boy got possession of a pin—a rather scarce article in that neighborhood—and at one of the most fervent parts of the preacher's prayer stuck it into the lad sitting in front of him. The punctured youth gave a yell which could not be construed into an Amen on account of the petition. It raised the lad off his seat, and made him jump forward with an impetus which was both amusing and pathetic. The hurt of the pin seemed to swallow up every feeling save that of distress, and he "boo-hooed" aloud.

Such proceedings made Brother Larkin bring his prayer to an abrupt conclusion, and Viola LeMonde hurried to the sobbing child, and tried to comfort him.

After the devotions the school was divided into classes. John Larkin took the adults of both sexes; Viola LeMonde, the larger girls; Henrietta Harvey, the smaller; George LeMonde, the older boys; and Stella Nebeker, the younger.

These teachers that day occupied places of responsibility which taxed every particle of their skill, ingenuity, tact, patience and forbearance. Many of those sitting around them could not read or write a word. So first they had to be taught words and sentences. Their knowledge of the Bible was pitifully small. Yet they possessed the redeeming feature of wanting to learn, and most of them showed an eager desire to improve their minds.

Let us, as unbidden guests, in spirit sit down in Viola LeMonde's class and listen to what is said. These girls' minds were bright but undeveloped. It was their teacher's object to educate—lead out—her pupils' intellects into the broad fields of Scriptural knowledge.

"Girls," said Viola, "we are going to study the book, copies of which we are holding in our hands. It is called the Bible. Let me ask some questions about it, and you try to answer them."

"Have you seen the Bible before today?"

Susanna Spink replied: "I seed one onct, when I went to a camp meetin' near Honey Crick. A man read out of a book he called de Bible, and then he talked and talked a long, long time."

"The Bible tells us a lot about many good men and women. Perhaps you have heard of some of these. Who was Moses?"

"Was he nigger Mose's dad?" asked one of the girls.

"No, he lived many years ago, and was a great leader of the Hebrew people. Did you ever hear of David?"

Profound silence.

"He was a mighty king of the Jews, and also a man who

Edward T. Curnick

wrote many beautiful songs. One of his songs millions of children know. It begins: 'The Lord is my shepherd; I shall not want.' Have any of you ever heard it?"

One or two raised their hands indicating they had heard it.

"Let us turn to it, the twenty-third psalm, and we shall read it together."

This they did, and Viola said: "I want you children to learn this psalm by heart and each one say it to me next Sunday. Will you do it?"

Every hand was raised in consent.

"The Bible is divided into two parts. Can any one tell me what they are?"

"Yes'm, de front an' de back."

"They are called the Old Testament and the New Testament. The Old Testament tells of God's dealings with his chosen people the Hebrews (or Jews). It also points to the coming of God's Son into the world."

"The New Testament tells how God's Son Jesus Christ came upon earth to be the Friend of little children and all people; how he lived a good life, always helping those around him; how wicked men at last put him to death, and his friends buried him. But the grave could not hold him, and on the third day he arose from it, and soon went up to heaven. The day of his birth is called Christmas. Have you heard of it?"

"Yes, teacher, we have all heard something about Christmas."

"Well, well learn more about it, for it is a sweet story, and next Christmas the mission school will have a fine time, with songs, and pieces to speak, and giving of presents. I hope my girls will take part in this glad time."

Thus the minutes sped by while in simple words Viola tried to impart some Bible truths to her willing scholars.

After closing exercises the school was dismissed.

The teachers remained a while to compare notes. George LeMonde reported having had an interesting time with his boys. He said he spoke to them about the sin of making moonshine whisky, and tried to set them against the practice. He was surprised at the answer that was made to one of his questions: "If any one were to ask you to take a drink of moonshine whisky, what would you say?"

"Thank you," piped up a small boy.

The first session of the Mission Sunday School was considered a success and those responsible for it were encouraged to continue the work.

Some change in the teaching force was necessary, for John Larkin's duties as preacher would not permit him to serve as a permanent teacher.

It is a pleasure to say that this school increased in numbers and influence, and not only in its Sunday meeting, but also in its social and educational work in the community, became a strong agent to uplift the surrounding hill people in every way.

Edward T. Curnick

CHAPTER XI

A KENTUCKY FEUD

Costello Nebeker after his conversion in his dance hall under the ministry of Jasper Very continued to keep his tavern, but discarded the sale and use of whisky upon his premises. He became known as the one hotel keeper in all that region who did not furnish his customers strong liquors. However, this action did not ruin his business; for, while some of his patrons left him, others took their places, and he was able still to supply all proper needs of the traveling public.

The winter had set in, and a great change was visible in the landscape. The splendid forest trees had lost their leaves, and their giant limbs were bare in the winter sunshine. A light snow covered the ground, and in it could be seen the tracks of rabbit, squirrel, coon, opossum, and occasionally a wild cat. In the distance the loud baying of hounds told that some creatures of the wild were being pursued by their relentless enemies.

Nature was at rest, and also the pioneer. His crops of corn, hay, wheat, tobacco, and vegetables were all gathered and safely placed in barns and storehouses. Little was to be done during the short winter day but to attend to the stock, to do the "chores" about the house, and perhaps to haul wood—

backlogs and foresticks—to replenish the ravenous fire in the great fireplace.

But what was a time of rest to the Kentucky farmer was a season of special activity to the pioneer preacher. It was usually in winter that "protracted meetings" were held. Next to camp meetings, they were the great religious events of the year. The old saints anticipated with keen relish the sermons, songs, prayers, exhortations, and altar services. The young people were scarcely less interested, but from mixed motives—partly religious and partly social. Ever since Adam courted Eve under Eden's trees God's woods have been places for lovers to woo in, and one of the best things connected with the "protracted meeting" was the occasion it made of bringing young people into one another's society and starting friendships which ripened into love and matrimony.

Through the influence of Costello Nebeker a small church was built some distance from his house in the noble forest. It was composed of logs cut smooth with axes on two opposite sides. These logs were placed one above the other, and the chinks between were closed up with mortar made of clay and water. The roof was of heavy beams upon which were nailed coarse clapboards. The building could boast of two small windows and a single door. The inside arrangements were as simple as the outside. A common wooden desk answered as a pulpit, and instead of pews wooden benches were placed in front of the stand. A large cast-iron stove, placed near the center of the room, gave heat when the weather was cold. The building was called the "Bethlehem Church."

The "protracted meeting" was appointed to begin early in January. The preachers who were to conduct it were Jasper Very, John Larkin, and Ezra Thompson, an old minister, grizzled and toughened by time and exposure.

This history has to do with the Sunday evening service which Jasper Very was to conduct. It was a beautiful winter evening. The orb of day had scarcely descended behind the unbroken line of forest trees in the west ere the full moon appeared in the east, rising in majesty through the trees. The silvery globe stretched from the base almost to the tops of the trees. Slowly and serenely she climbed on her upward way, the tree tops now marking the line of her diameter; then in a few minutes she was free from their obstruction and hung above the earth a great, shining ball, sending upon river, forest, plain, and plantation a light so full and soft that one standing in it would become charmed by her magical rays.

In the falling darkness it was easy to walk or ride to the evening appointment. Because of the distance most of the people rode on horseback. When they had all assembled, the sight was one to remember. Horses were hitched everywhere to racks which had been placed near the church, to branches of trees, and to small saplings.

Before the services began many of the people had gathered inside the church, which was illuminated with a half dozen tallow candles that tried their best to burn, but seemed discouraged by the attempt. Outside men collected in groups and talked in low, earnest tones. Do you ask what was the subject of their conversation? It was about the sermon to be preached that night by Jasper Very.

A few days before a family feud in this neighborhood had broken out afresh. It was the noted feud between the Wiles and Barker families. This estrangement had occurred a quarter of a century before. It began by some cattle of a former Wiles getting into the field of a settler named Barker. Barker told Wiles to keep his live stock out of his land, and Wiles replied by demanding that Barker should repair his rail fences and mind his gates. Wiles was careless about his cattle and Barker about his fences. So one night a lot of Wiles' cattle got into a fine field of growing corn belonging to Barker, and ate as long as they could chew the juicy food and trampled down the green stalks with perfect indifference as to ownership. Early the next morning Barker saw the devastation and the causes thereof. He walked over to Wiles' plantation, and the two men quarreled, fought, and almost killed each other.

This was the beginning of that celebrated Wiles-Barker feud which has soiled the annals of that part of Kentucky. Its course was marked by murders, assassinations, wounds, burning of buildings, and every injury which cunning could devise and hate execute.

For a full year before this winter, by an unspoken agreement, the two factions had ceased to quarrel. Violence had exhausted itself, for the worst of men cannot give loose rein to their passions all the time. But, though the wild beast of hatred and revenge was quiet, he was neither dead nor changed into a lamb; he was really nursing and strengthening his powers for more savage attacks. The occasion which made him crouch, show his teeth, and leap forward with sudden and terrible fury was a barn-raising on a settler's farm not far from Costello's tavern. The Wiles and Barker families were both well represented by young and middle-aged men. According to the custom of the time, whisky was freely tendered to the workers and as freely received.

All went well until late in the afternoon when the framework of the barn had been put in place. The settlers had drunk unusual quantities of their favorite beverage, and were ready for frolic or fight. Just then Alan Barker, a scion of the noted family, belonging to that branch living in Pigeon Creek, began expatiating on the charms, graces and virtues of a fair

Edward T. Curnick

lassie bearing the euphonious and patriotic name of America Virginia Stubbins, and closed his eulogy by saying she was "de sweetest, prettiest, best and likeliest gal in all Kentuck," and he could "whip any man in de crowd who dared to deny it." Young "Buck" Wiles took up the dare, partly because he despised the whole Barker crew, partly because he had a tender feeling toward the same lass, and was therefore jealous of Alan Barker, but mostly because whisky had fired his brain. So he discounted Alan Barker's fervid descriptions, and averred that the same America Virginia Stubbins possessed a homely face and little sense.

This was the spark which exploded the magazine. Alan Barker, stung to anger and madness, sprang upon "Buck" Wiles, and the two men clenched in a desperate struggle. However, it was not the way of the times to confine the settling of disputes to the "manly art" of bare fists. There was a quicker method, and sooner than we can write it the men having become separated in their wrestling, Alan Barker whipped out a pistol and shot Wiles down. Then ensued an encounter horrible to relate. The members of each family entered at once into the fight. Many shots were exchanged; and after a few minutes, when the fighting was over, either from lack of ammunition, or because, Indian fashion, those who were not wounded had hidden behind the great trees to fight from under cover, the sad results were apparent. Three of the Barker tribe and two of the Wiles lay dead upon the ground, while five of the latter and four of the former were lying in different positions, some slightly, others desperately, wounded.

Thus the old feud was renewed, the old score opened, and the waters of malice, revenge and hate which had been accumulating for months broke forth afresh with devastating effect. Soon the news was heard in all the surrounding hills and valleys. It stirred the dull and untrained minds in many a mountain cabin; it was discussed between drinks in rough taverns. Somehow the story sounded through the green Kentucky woods until its echoes appeared in the daily papers of Cincinnati, Philadelphia and New York.

Jasper Very declared he would make this battle between families the subject of his sermon on Sunday evening, and it was this announcement which threw the neighborhood into such a high state of excitement and caused a crowd to attend the meeting which packed the small meeting-house to suffocation and, despite the cold weather, caused it to overflow into the surrounding yard.

Sam Wiles was there, and his impish shadow, Zibe Turner, and Long Tom, and the rest of his cronies. Sam Wiles' family was a part of that large Wiles faction which warred with the Barkers, but Sam was not present at the barn-raising. He was only fourth cousin to the Wiles men who were killed, but felt himself bound with the rest of his kin to avenge their death. Hence he was intensely interested to know how the preacher would treat his subject. On account of the crowd he sat a little within the doorway, while the monster dwarf contented himself with a position just outside, where his ghoulish and malignant face was lighted up by candle rays and moonbeams combined.

Jasper Very took for his text, "Am I my brother's keeper?" Thus he began: "Hearers and friends, it is a sad fact that the first man born into the world, Cain, was a murderer, and the second man born of woman was murdered. Cain killed his brother Abel. Ever since that day this earth has been reddened with human blood. It has defiled every mountain and stained every plain, it has polluted the waters of every lake and river, and has reddened the very ocean. Murder's bloody hand, nerved by all the worst passions of man, has struck down, not only the guilty, but also the innocent, the

Edward T. Curnick

weak and helpless. It is a perversion of the Creator's intention regarding mankind. He made men to dwell in peace and happiness. He put the solitary in families that each member might contribute to the well-being of the whole. Every man is his brother's keeper. He is expected to do him good and not harm. If my brother is weak, I must try to be his strength. If he is in sorrow, I must comfort him; if needy, help him with my substance; if sick, I must minister unto him. By so doing I shall receive both the approval of my conscience, and the Master's reward: 'Well done, good and faithful servant.'

"Back of the act of murder is its motive. It is formed in the mind before it is committed by the hand. It invariably springs from the baser passions of man—hate, malice, jealousy, revenge. Our Bible traces it to its seat. It declares: 'Whosoever hateth his brother is a murderer: and ye know that no murderer hath eternal life abiding in him.' It was this bad feeling of hate which made Cain kill his brother Abel."

The preacher then passed on to say: "You all know that different parts of our beautiful State of Kentucky have been disgraced by family feuds which have resulted in many crimes against God and man, including murder. In our own neighborhood at this time of the year when we should be making fresh resolutions of love to God and our fellows, young men have shot one another down in a useless quarrel, a number of families are mourning the loss of sons and brothers, and other men are made cripples for life by ugly wounds."

Then, raising his voice until it could be heard by the remotest lounger at the horserails he thundered: "What was the cause of this recent killing, and of the broils, fights, and contentions in our midst? Whisky. This is the curse of Kentucky. It is the demon which fires the blood and pulls the trigger. In days when the red men roamed these forests and hunted abundant game so many battles were fought among themselves that this fair land received that dreadful name, 'The Dark and Bloody Ground,' and now you are doing all in your power to perpetuate this name. You in this audience who make or sell liquor, either legally or illegally, 'have made a covenant with death, and with hell are at agreement.' How can you escape the wrath of God? The voice of these slain men's blood cries unto heaven from the ground. The gray hairs of their parents will go down in sorrow to the grave for them."

His mood and voice then changed, and in softer tones he pleaded with them to turn from the evil of their ways and live. He assured them that no drunkard nor drunkard-maker could inherit the kingdom of God, that a sure woe would rest upon him who putteth the bottle to his neighbor's lips, and that no good could finally come out of this bad business. He told them that they could not turn from their evil ways in their own strength; but God had laid strength upon One who was mighty to save and strong to deliver from every weakness and temptation, even his only begotten Son, Jesus Christ.

His eyes filled with tears and his voice shook with emotion as he gave an invitation to all to forsake their sins and return unto God in that sweetest welcome to repent that human ears have heard: "Come unto me, all ye that labor and are heavy laden, and I will give you rest."

Almost overcome by his feelings, Jasper Very sat down, but instantly John Larkin arose and gave out that comforting invitation hymn:

"Come, ye sinners, poor and needy,
Weak and wounded, sick and sore;
Jesus ready stands to save you,

Full of pity, love, and power.
He is able,
He is willing, doubt no more."

He asked all those who wanted to repent of their sins and to seek pardon and peace to come forward to the altar while the congregation stood and sang that hymn.

The result was astonishing. In spite of the crowded condition of the room men and women pushed their way to the wooden benches called an "altar," and with tears and groans sought forgiveness. Decisions were made that night as lasting as eternity. Many a hardened backwoods sinner there forever forsook his evil ways and became an order-loving and respectable citizen, helping to form that civilization of which the Kentucky of today is so proud. Several moonshiners were convicted of the iniquity of their business, and gave up illicit distilling and their other bad practices. Among the rest was Long Tom. He sought the Lord with the simplicity of a little child. As he made no reservations, but at once confessed all his evil deeds, and was both wise and simple enough to accept Christ at his own terms of full surrender and childlike faith, he soon found pardon and peace. While he bowed at the altar the people sang "Jesus Lover of My Soul," and its sentiments comforted the sobbing man. The clearest voice which led in this hymn was that of Viola LeMonde.

At a testimony meeting a short time after he told of his experience: "Friends, I war a mighty ignorant feller when I come for'ard to that mourner's bench. I had not said a prayer for twenty years. I did not know how to begin. Then I thought of a prayer my mother larned me when I war a little chap. So I began saying, 'Our Father, who art in heaven,' and before I got through I war saved."

But while some were convicted of the error of their ways at that meeting, others were hardened; for such a meeting is either a savior of life unto life, or a savior of death unto death. Sam Wiles sat, as we have said, near the open door. During the first part of the discourse he followed the preacher closely and calmly; but when Jasper Very entered upon his philippic against the moonshiners in particular, an awful struggle began in Wiles' heart. God's Spirit acted strongly upon him, convincing his judgment that all the preacher said was true, that the whole business was bad from beginning to end, and that now, after he had such proofs among his own kin that death followed in its wake, he should forever abandon it. For a while it seemed as though his proud heart would yield, but there were tremendous influences on the other side. There was the love of his free and easy life which must be put in the scale. If he changed about he must endure the scoffs and reproaches of his former companions. Added to these was the awful tug of the habits and inclinations of his present life, and beyond all this was the personal temptation of the evil one whispering in his soul not to yield. If he did yield, said the tempter, he would soon fall away, and that would be worse than not to start at all.

Thus the crucial battle of his life was fought while Wiles sat in that little church. Such a struggle comes into many a life. Angels must look upon it with the deepest interest and attention. The crisis may arrive at church or at home, on the high sea or on the land, in a storied mansion or in a little cottage, at the midnight hour or in the open day—the place or time counts for little, but the result is as wide as eternity.

This hour was propitious for Sam Wiles. A proper choice would have revolutionized his character, would have gladdened the angels in heaven, and written his name deep in the "Book of Life." But alas! alas! before the sermon was ended he had resisted God's Holy Spirit, and, instead of one devil, seven devils had entered into his soul. A hard expression spread over his face, his eyes flashed with a dangerous fire, and he cast a look of defiance and contempt upon the speaker that (so subtle, strong, and swift are the laws of mind) Very, seeing it, would have been confused and perhaps overcome in his discourse if the shield of Almighty God had not protected him.

As for Zibe Turner, the monster dwarf, the services had no more effect for good upon him than a strong fortress would be affected by shooting white beans at it. When his favorite business, illicit distilling, was denounced by Very, the dwarf's wrath grew so hot that he could not refrain from muttering under his breath: "I wish I could drown you uns and all yer pious hypercrits in whisky. Dat's my holt."

As the last hymn was being sung Sam Wiles left the church and walked out into the moonlight. He was joined by Turner and a few more of the clan. For a few minutes they held a whispered conversation, and then separated.

When the meeting broke up a half hour later, it was found that the girths on the horses belonging to the preachers, the Costello family and others had been cut and destroyed. Also the traces of Judge LeMonde's harness.

CHAPTER XII

THE SHAMEFUL PLOT

The moonlight showed a look of blank amazement and concern upon the faces of the victims of this dastardly trick, especially the women; but John Larkin's unfailing good temper and witty sayings relieved the situation. "There is no use crying over spilled milk," said he, "and I am sure, as Poor Richard remarks, 'God helps them that help themselves.' So we must find some way to remedy this trouble, for we cannot stand here gazing into the moon's face all night, and the distance to our homes is too great to walk. Let us look about among the trees, and perhaps we can find pieces of the girths and harness."

This was done, and presently several pieces were found. With these the traces of the carriage were repaired and a number of the saddles made fit for service. By some of the men riding double on horseback the mischief was tolerably mended and all returned to their lodgings in safety.

While one injury was being remedied another more serious was being planned. When Sam Wiles and Zibe Turner had cut the saddle girths and traces, they and three of their pals quickly mounted their horses and rode rapidly to Wiles' house. Arriving there they found the old folks and children in bed. Being afraid to talk over their infamous scheme in the cabin, they betook themselves to the barn some distance away. In this building they lighted a tallow dip and, throwing themselves down on some hay to rest and warm their bodies, they at once began talking of what was uppermost in their minds.

"Now fellers," said Wiles, "let us go over keerfully what we uns war sayin' as we rode along. That cursed preacher made a last break with me when he fit our bizness in such an all-fired strong way and throwed insults on my family. I say he oughter be punished for his sass in the way we spoke of."

"Sure nuff," broke in Turner, the monster dwarf, "tar and feathers and ridin' in a rail is too good fer de likes of him. If he got his just dues, we oughter lay for him some night and pick him off as he is ridin' hossback."

"We must not kill him," said the more cautious leader, "for they would 'spect us at once, and we would soon be put in de jug (jail), if they didn't make us stretch hemp without trial. But a good thick coat of tar and feathers will become his style of beauty fust-rate; and if we uns ride him on a rail, he will dance a jig with his feet in de air and will look more cute than ary Injun you uns ever see daubed with his war paint and feathers."

The five men laughed heartily at this remark, and seemed to anticipate with delight the fulfillment of their foul plot.

"We owe him a good one fer capturin' Long Tom and makin' him pious and an enemy of our bizness," said Bert Danks, captain of the Honey Crick band, "and I hope you uns won't be sparin' of de tar ner easy with de rail. Get one of them three-cornered hickory rails, and that'll do the thing up brown."

"Whar is de best place to s'prise him?" asked Wiles.

"I'll tell yer," spoke Zibe Turner, and his monkeyish face lit up with a smile almost diabolical and his piercing black eyes shot a keen and excited look into the group, "I hearn that he has an appintment next Chewsday night at de top of Bald Knob, and to go there from his home he will have to take de Pigeon Crick road, cross de crick at Farley's and then branch off inter de big woods before he climbs de knob. Now de level place jest by de foot of de knob is a lonely spot, away from de big road, de trees air mighty high and large, and few people pass that way. I say let's strip and dress him thar."

"Agreed!" shouted the rest in concert.

"Bert," spoke Wiles, "we'll look to you to git de tar, and I'll bring a pot from mammy's kitchen to heat it in. I'll also take without her knowin' it some feathers from her feather bed. You, Zibe, are to furnish de rail, and see that you git a sharp and strong one."

"'Pend on me for dat, and if he don't cry for marcy, it'll not be my fault."

As a parting caution Wiles remarked: "All you fellers keep mum on this subject, for we don't want to miss de fun ner be cotched in it."

Now it happened that Mose Williams, Judge LeMonde's most faithful negro servant, was attending to an affair of his own that Sunday evening not strictly demanded by his obligations to his master. In other words, he was courting a sprightly and good-looking quadroon girl, by name Euphemia Jackson ("Femy" for short). This buxom lass was a house servant on a plantation situated about five miles from Judge LeMonde's. What were five miles to a lusty

Edward T. Curnick

young negro fellow who had a good pair of legs, a bracing atmosphere and bright moonlight in which to exercise them, and a sweetheart at the journey's end?

Mose, arrayed in his best clothes, had gone early and stayed late. He left the plantation happy with himself and all the world. For had he not that very night popped the all-important question and had not Femy given an answer which warmed the very depths of his darkey heart and made the face of nature shine with a double light? To shorten the distance home, as the hour was late and the bright moon threw some light even among the thick trees, he determined to take a footpath among the hills. This course led him close to the cabin of Simon Wiles, Sam Wiles' father. He was walking in a zigzag path, now watching the moonlight as it lilted down through the leafy canopy, making a dim but peaceful light around him; now listening to the sounds which exist in Kentucky forests in winter, the flight of nocturnal birds and moving of animals; seeing the raccoon crossing his track like a shadow in search of food; hearing the mournful hooting of owls in various directions.

Suddenly he was startled by seeing a light shining through the chinks of a building. At once Mose determined to discover its meaning. He had no fine-spun theories as to the wrong of eavesdropping. Besides, there might be robbers planning to steal neighbor Wiles' horse or produce. So he crept up to the barn, making so little noise that neither the watchful dogs nor the plotting men heard him.

He arrived in time to hear the conversation we have recorded. When he had learned all, he stealthily retraced his steps to the foot-path and, making a wide detour around the house, went on his way. While he walked he thus soliloquized: "Ho! Ho! dat's yo' game, is it? Well, dis niggah will try to spile yo' purty plan. But, Mose, ef yo' squeal on dem men an' dey hears about it, dey'll give yo' wusser t'ings dan tar an' fedders. Kain't help dat; mus' run de resk. Mas'r Very am mighty pop'lar wid de Jedge, and I believes dat Miss Viola am lookin' on him wid more'n common feelin's. Mose, yo's gwine to be a married man one of dese days yo'self, an' yo' wants a little cabin of yo' own; and ef yo' hoe dis row to de end an' circumwent dese 'spiring men, p'haps Mas'r LeMonde gwine give yo' de cabin an' Miss Viola gwine put lots o' nice tings in it. Dat's de proposition; an', Mose, yo' got to keep yo' wooly head mighty cool an' calc'lating. Chewsday will soon be hyar, an' what is done mus' be done in a hurry. It's a pity de Jedge an' Mas'r George is gwine to start early to Lexinton tomorrer, so dey can't 'tend to de mattah; but I'll jes inform Miss Viola of de situwation."

When the slave had reached this wise and satisfactory conclusion he had also reached the end of his journey, and with much self-complacency retired to his humble cot to dream of his dusky sweetheart.

Early the next morning Mose called at the mansion to see Miss Viola, telling her that he had "sumpin' of special 'portance" to make known. For the sake of privacy, she took him into the large drawing-room and, seating herself in that beautiful bay window overlooking the stately lawn and the broad cornfield now shining white under their coverlet of snow and farther on the lovely river, she beckoned him to proceed. With much earnestness and an air of importance he related what he had heard at the barn the night before.

Mose was so absorbed in his recital that he did not notice the full effects of his words on his mistress. As his story continued, a great change came over her. Her breathing quickened until it came in short and labored gasps. First a deeper color of red suffused her cheeks, then a crimson overspread her face and neck, which was soon followed by a

Edward T. Curnick

paleness which marked her face with an ashen hue. How that poor heart was troubled! Now its violent beatings force the hot blood to face and hands and feet; then with the cruel news it takes into itself the torrid currents of blood, leaving the face and extremities cold and bloodless and a feeling of suffocation in the lungs. By a supreme effort of will, which God has made sovereign over the emotions, she calmed her beating heart and considered what was best to be done.

"Mose, you are quite sure you have told me all you heard?"

"Yes, Miss Viola, I is, kase de wo'ds made such a 'pression on mah mind dat I 'members dem zackly."

"You are certain they selected Tuesday night for their wicked acts?"

"Dey spoke of Chewsday night, and tuk it bekase Mas'r Very is to go dat way dat night."

"You can leave me now for an hour, but at eight o'clock come back and I will send by you a message to Mr. Very."

When the negro had left, Viola LeMonde retired to her own room and seating herself at her writing desk, wrote the following communication:

"Mount Pisgah, January 6, 181—.

The Rev. Jasper Very,

Dear Mr. Very:

Our servant, Mose Williams, has just made known to me a plot which some base men have devised to treat you with indignity and to bring the cause of religion into contempt. Mose was returning home late last night from Mr. St. Claire's plantation when, seeing a light in Simon Wiles' barn, he crept near and, looking through a chink in the wall, saw Sam Wiles, Bert Danks, Zibe Turner, and two other men lying on some hay. He overheard them planning to administer to Rev. Jasper Very a coat of tar and feathers and to complete the performance by riding him on a rail. This disgraceful act is to take place next Tuesday night. The spot is that dark and unfrequented place at the foot of Bald Knob through which you must pass on the way to your preaching service.

"As 'to be forewarned is to be forearmed,' I hasten to notify you of the plot, feeling sure you will adopt measures to thwart it. Father and George would aid you in the matter but they went early this morning to Lexington, and will not return till Wednesday evening.

"I feel that I am able to do little in such an emergency as this; but if I can be of any help, I will most gladly endeavor to preserve the respect of our community and to assist a friend.

"No one knows of this plot except the instigators, myself, and Mose. By him I send this note to you.

Most sincerely yours,

Viola LeMonde."

At eight o'clock Mose made his appearance, and Viola gave him the message, telling him to ride Velox as fast as possible to Mr. Nebeker's tavern, where Mr. Very had spent the night, and to give it to the preacher.

Edward T. Curnick

Mose was doubly willing that the news should get to the parson by means of the note; for if trouble came his way, he could swear that he did not inform Very of the plot; and, secondly, he thought Viola would be pleased to help the preacher.

Jasper Very was still at the home of the tavern keeper, as were also several other preachers, including the "square man," John Larkin. Jasper was standing on the porch, and was surprised to see the colored man riding up fast to the house, his horse wet with sweat and steaming in the wintry air.

Mose, dismounting, lifted his cap to those present, and said to Jasper Very: "I has a message of 'portance to you, sir." With this he handed him the note, and then, on request of Mr. Nebeker, put Velox in the barn to cool off and rest.

Jasper Very took the missive to the end of the porch and, breaking the seal, read it. When he had finished, his mobile face showed the conflicting emotions within. A flush of anger reddened his dark features, his lips were pressed close together, his eyes flashed with unwonted fire, and his hands involuntarily became clenched until the finger nails indented the palms. Soon his look softened, the fire left his eyes, and they appeared as gentle as twin lakes in lovely Switzerland. The proud lines in his lips gave place to a curve like a Cupid's bow and a smile lighted up his face. Looking out over the wintry landscape, he said to himself: "It is worth the danger of an attack like this to receive such a note from Viola LeMonde. How kind and thoughtful of her to warn me of the plot so quickly. I will see how best I can circumvent this scheme." With these reflections he retraced his steps to his friends.

In the meantime the pity which Viola LeMonde felt for the preacher did not tend to weaken that strange sensation, born in Eden, which was tugging at her heart.

Edward T. Curnick

CHAPTER XIII

INTO A PIT (OR PITCH)

Jasper very addressed Costello Nebeker, the tavern keeper, thus: "Brother Nebeker, I have a matter of importance to consider with you and a few friends. Can you furnish us with a private room?"

"Certainly, Brother Very," replied his genial host. "You can have the sitting-room, just back of our large reception-room." (The dance hall had been changed into these two rooms.)

In a few minutes a select company was gathered there. It consisted of Jasper Very, John Larkin, Ezra Thompson, the old, grizzled preacher, Nathaniel Grimes, a smart minister who formerly had been a lawyer, Costello Nebeker, and his wife. Jasper Very read Viola LeMonde's note to the group, and striking was the effect it produced. One cried, "The despicable villains!" another, "The vile sinners." a third, "Shame on Kentucky manhood, to what depths can humanity sink!" For once John Larkin could not find a quotation from Poor Richard or any other source which met the case. But soon surprise and indignation gave way to a cool consideration of the situation and the best means of circumventing this well-laid plot and bringing its instigators to punishment.

Very was the first to offer a suggestion. "Friends," he said, "let us call Mose into the room and hear in detail his account of what he overheard." This was thought good advice, and accordingly Mose was invited into the sitting-room.

At first the cautious darkey was loath to commit himself; but when he was informed that Miss LeMonde already had told the tale in substance and that all present, would keep secret his remarks, he repeated what he had seen and heard with more fullness than we have written down.

After Mose had been dismissed, Nathaniel Grimes, the lawyer-preacher, spoke in these words: "I believe I have a plan by which this plot can be frustrated. It is this: Let Brother Very prepare for his journey tomorrow as though nothing unusual was expected; let us notify two or more constables to enter the woods from a different direction just after dark tomorrow evening, and at a convenient distance from where the plotters post themselves behind great trees. Let Friend Nebeker, Brother Larkin, and myself steal into the woods as best we can and join the constables in season. At the proper time let Brother Very ride slowly along, and when he is met by the ruffians and the parley takes place, we will suddenly rush upon the scene and capture them in their base act."

The plan was discussed for some time and, being found simple and practicable, was adopted. Costello Nebeker was to engage the services of the constables. Being a layman, he could do so without exciting suspicion.

Tuesday evening the sky was partly covered with clouds. About the time Jasper Very started from his home the moon rose in beauty. Sometimes she threw the full glory of her beams upon the white earth as she rode in a clear place in the heavens; at others her light was obscured by passing clouds

Edward T. Curnick

which covered her fair face. We can follow the gospel ranger as he left his humble boarding place.

Mounted on trustworthy Bob, Jasper Very started to his appointment. He turned his horse's head toward the east and rode for half a mile along a farm road when, coming to a gate, he opened it and came into a broader county road. Just opposite this gate stood the immense barn on Judge LeMonde's estate, in which was stored his hay and grain and in which were kept his many horses. Up a gradual ascent a few hundred feet beyond stood the Judge's mansion. The man of God gazed upon it as its outlines were visible in the moonlight. He thought of the fair daughter who lived there and who had taken such an interest in his welfare. Was it fact or fancy which showed him a female figure dressed in white standing by the west bay window? The distance was too great to see clearly; but perhaps that intercommunication of minds which in later times we call telepathy was the thing which caused his heart to beat with a stronger stroke and fired his spirit with greater courage.

Yes, there was a woman's form standing at that window. Viola was watching for Jasper to pass along. Her white face was pressed against the window pane, and she strained her eyes to see. Her effort was rewarded, for she could well perceive the outline of horse and man as they went along the road. Although Jasper had sent a reply to her note by Moses, thanking her for her interest in his welfare and telling her of the conference at the tavern, with a woman's supersensi-tiveness she was most anxious as to the result; and as she saw him ride away into danger, she put her hand to her heart and, raising her eyes to heaven, prayed most fervently that he might be protected from harm.

Jasper Very proceeded on his way along the country road. Soon he passed the little schoolhouse on his right, then

Bethlehem Church on his left. Next he crossed the rude bridge spanning the brook, and rode on a half mile farther. Leaving the large road, he turned to the left, going northwest through the deep woods toward the base of Bald Knob.

As he neared the spot selected for the attack he heard faint whistles on both sides of the road which were signals before agreed upon that his aids were present. Passing along to the place where he knew the outlaws were concealed, he began singing a camp meeting hymn.

Suddenly the ruffians sprang from the roadside, one seizing his horse's bridle, who proved to be Bert Danks.

"Good evenin', parson, you uns seem to be in a happy frame of mind, or air ye singin' to keep yer courage up?" The speaker was Sam Wiles, who was holding his right boot.

"Much courage is not needed when a man is among friends or cowards, and you must be one or the other," replied Very.

"We'll show yer what sort of friends we air," spoke up Zibe Turner; "so jest obleege we uns by gittin' down off'n that 'er hoss, or we'll help yer down."

"I have an engagement up the knob tonight, and I have not time to tarry with you now," said the preacher.

"Well, parson, we uns have fixed up a leetle meetin' on our own account, and there ain't much singin' nor prayin' in it, nuther. I reckon we'll pay yer back for tryin' to spile our bizness and hurt our reputations. If you won't come down far (fair), we uns must help yer off," growled Turner.

"Men, I seem to be in your power, and surely I would rather dismount of my own accord than be pulled off." With these

Edward T. Curnick

words Very threw his foot over Bob's back and lighted on the ground.

Instantly he was surrounded by Wiles, Turner, and two other ruffians. Bert Danks still held Bob by the bit.

Very looked about him as best he could, and saw a smouldering fire beneath a large pot. In this pot was a large quantity of tar which had been somewhat heated to soften it, and close by lay a gunny bag containing feathers, while still beyond was a long fence rail which had been taken from a zigzag fence not far away.

"Now, if you'll be so kind, please take off yer preacher's coat and shirt; and if you find de weather too cold for comfort, we uns will put on anudder coat which will keep out de air," remarked Wiles.

"A matter of necessity need not be discussed," said the traveler, and with this remark he pulled off his long clerical outer garment.

Very did this for a double purpose: first, to free himself from incumbrance when he needed to use his arms; and, secondly, by removing suspicion of resistance, to take his enemies off their guard.

No sooner had he slipped his coat off than he gave a loud whistle, and shooting out his right fist with all his strength, struck Wiles squarely on the jaw and sent him sprawling on the ground several feet away. This was the beginning of a strenuous fight. The moment his chief was knocked down Zibe Turner, the monster dwarf, sprang upon Very, and putting one of his apelike arms around his neck, cried: "Dat's my holt." With the other arm he began hitting the parson about the head and body. At the same time the other men were trying to throw him off his feet. Very, knowing help was near at hand, made almost superhuman efforts to stand his ground, though he was half suffocated and stunned by the dwarf's hug and blows.

Very's whistle was answered by a shout down the road, and almost instantly the forms of five men appeared. The outlaws, though surprised, were not panic-stricken, and they met the attack of the constables and preachers with reckless bravery. For a quarter of an hour things were in a strange mix-up. Wiles, rising from the ground, was making for Very, when a burly constable hurrying up caught the outlaw and together they fell squirming, rolling, twisting, fighting over the ground.

Another officer made a break for Bert Danks. Letting go of Bob's bridle, he clenched with his man, and they were fighting like two possessed. Nathaniel Grimes, the great red-headed, raw-boned, lawyer-preacher, was as good in a fight as in an argument and, striking one of the ruffians, gave a good account of himself. John Larkin had to try conclusions with another culprit, and they were at it, give and take, like the rest. In like manner Nebeker did his part.

The officer of the law who grappled with Sam Wiles was one of the strongest men in the county and, despite Wiles' prowess and desperate fighting, the constable soon had him mastered and clapped handcuffs on him.

In the meantime Jasper Very and the monster dwarf were having an interesting combat. Turner would not relax his hold upon his adversary in spite of all he could do. His grip on his throat was like a coil of the cobra de capello. At first Very was at the mercy of the dwarf; and if things had gone on this way a little longer serious consequences would have come to the preacher. Though he was half choked by the

Edward T. Curnick

other's arm, Very, summoning all his strength, took hold of his antagonists's arm and pulled it from his throat. Then, lifting his enemy in his arms, he threw him with violence from him. Very was not particular in which direction the ugly man should go nor the spot on which he should alight. The fates decreed a bitter punishment, for the dwarf came plump into the pot of warm tar which had been prepared for the preacher. Turner was wedged in the pot, so that he could not extricate himself, and meantime the thick fluid beneath was making a warm acquaintance with his trousers and legs. This unlooked-for disgrace and undoing of the two leaders brought the pitched battle to a close. The unknown rascals, having broken away from their antagonists and seeing the discomfiture of their chiefs, fled up the knob road, while the three principals, Wiles, Turner, Danks, were taken into custody.

The scene closes with John Larkin, a broad smile on his face, looking at the disconsolate Turner and saying: "He digged a pit, and is fallen into the ditch which he made."

CHAPTER XIV

RETURNING THANKS

The captors of these outlaws were more merciful than the rowdies, for Nathaniel Grimes went to a farmhouse not far away and borrowed some clothes to replace those tar-besmeared which Turner had on. When he had changed his garments the two constables and Nebeker conducted the prisoners on horseback to the county seat where they were locked up in jail.

In the meantime Jasper Very, John Larkin, and Nathaniel Grimes mounted their horses and made their way up Bald Knob to a little meetinghouse on its top where services were to be held. Very's encounter with the outlaws had made him late in reaching the church, which caused some surprise to those who had assembled, for they knew their pastor to be a very punctual man. However, he thought it best not to mention the cause of his delay. Simply remarking that he was unavoidably detained, he began the services.

Early the next morning our three friends started down the knob, Jasper Very to go to Judge LeMonde's house personally to thank Miss Viola for her part in helping him to avoid the trap set for him, and Larkin and Grimes to ride about fifteen miles down the river road to keep an engagement to

Edward T. Curnick

preach that night at a small hamlet called Bridgewater.

When Jasper Very dismounted at Judge LeMonde's barn gate, he was met by Mose Williams, who burst forth with loud and eager words: "Hi! Hi! Mas'r Very, ah knows dat yo' circumwented dem villians. Yo' don't ketch dis coon nappin'. I war a-layin' low las' night to see de outcome of dat amberscade, an' ah seed wid mah own eyes dat yo' won out."

"What did you see, Mose, and how did you see it?" asked the preacher.

"Ah war a-hidin' behin' de upper big post of de barn gate, an' ah hearn hosses' hoofs beatin' up de road, an' soon de constables cum along wid de prisoners. Wa'n't dem moonshiners mad, do? Jes' as dey war 'proaching de gate Sam Wiles said: 'Dat cantin' preacher has got me 'rested twice now, but he won't do it ag'in. Ah'll die 'fore ah'll let him beat me 'n'ur time.' An' den dat monkey, Zibe Turner, fell to cussin' yo' an' de constables an' de Jedge an' all de ch'ch people permiscus. He said, ef he knew de rascal what giv' de plot away, he would skin 'im alive an' hang up his skin in his back yard to skeer away de ghosts. He swore sich drefful oaths ah was afeered de trees by de roadside was gwine to fall on 'em. He mad mah blood run col', an' ah war pow'ful glad he didn't 'spect me."

"Well, Mose, you are safe for the present anyway, for these wicked men will be tried in court soon, and they will be sent to jail for quite a while. Now put my horse in a stall, for I am going to make a call at the big house."

Saying this, Jasper Very handed his bridle to Mose, and also gave him two bits in silver. He then passed through a second gate and walked toward the mansion, which was some two hundred yards distant. When he got near the door, Sport, king of all Judge LeMonde's hunting dogs, came bounding toward him, loudly barking. This great animal was dangerous to strangers but, knowing Very, he came up to him and licked his hand with his red tongue. Very spoke to him and admired his noble form—his high forehead, intelligent eyes, wide nostrils, deep chest, long yellow body, slim but muscular legs—then walked on to the front piazza and rang the doorbell.

While he is waiting there let us take a peep inside. Miss Viola LeMonde, by a law of mind not yet explained, had a premonition that a certain clergyman would visit her that morning. So she had a particular care as to her apparel. She called her faithful maidservant Nora to bring her a white dress, which had a faint shade of blue mixed with the white. This gown, which exactly fitted her shapely figure, she put on, and around her neck and wrists she placed soft and delicate ruching. Then she went to the flower conservatory and selecting a deep-red rosebud, placed it against some dark green leaves and pinned it to her dress. Her hair was formed at the back in a large knot of gold, while over her beautiful brows it was brushed smooth, giving her a look like a Madonna.

When Very rang the bell Viola was in the sitting-room to the right of the hall. Nora opened the door and invited him into the drawing-room at the left of the hall. With a perversity which no mere man understands, and we suppose is unaccountable to woman's mind, Viola would not at once greet the minister, but laid that duty upon her mother. In a minute or two Madame LeMonde, a stately dame in form and mien, worthy of the position she occupied, walked into the room and cordially shook hands with Mr. Very. "I am glad to see you this fine morning, Mr. Very," she said. "Did you escape the base designs of those wicked men last night! Viola told me of the plot they had laid to do you harm. I am sorry that my husband and son were away, that they could not help you in your need."

"Yes, Mrs. LeMonde, thanks to the timely warning that your good daughter sent me, I was able to thwart their evil purposes; and at this moment the ringleaders, Sam Wiles, Zibe Turner, and Harve Davis are in the county jail. I have called personally to thank your daughter for her kindness to me. Is she at home this morning?"

"She is, Mr. Very, and if you will excuse me, I will send her into the room."

By this time Viola had brought her perverse little heart into harmony with her real wish and, having quieted her nerves by a strong effort of will, she was ready to heed her mother's summons to enter the drawing-room. As she stepped across the threshold there was a moment of embarrassment during which neither spoke; but it was only for a moment, Jasper Very being too full of gratitude to remain long silent. "Miss Viola," he said, grasping her hand, "I have come this morning to thank you for your great kindness in apprising me of Sam Wiles' plot to injure me. I am under a thousand obligations to you for what you did."

"Do not speak of that, Mr. Very; it was a thing any friend would have done. But tell me whether or not you escaped from their intentions without any injury to yourself."

"Yes, thanks to your promptness, I was able to enlist some friends on my behalf, and with them and some officers of the law we were able to outwit the ruffians and beat them at their own game." He then laid before her in detail the events of the past night.

Viola listened with closest attention to the narrative. When

Jasper spoke of being surrounded by the outlaws and their threats, the color left her cheeks; but when he told how their enemies were overcome and the ludicrous predicament of Turner as he sat in the pot of tar, a sigh of relief escaped her lips, which was followed by a hearty laugh. However, her mood soon changed, and with a serious look coming into her blue eyes she said: "I am sure those moonshiners are a menace to our community. They are becoming more and more hardened and reckless. I fear that they will yet do some of us great injury. They doubtless hate papa, who has to sentence them to prison, and they are foes of all order-loving men and women in this region. As to Sam Wiles, I cannot bear to be near him. His very presence repels and frightens me. When he looked at me in church last Sunday night, I shuddered. It seemed as though a venomous snake had put its folds around my neck. Zibe Turner, called the monster dwarf, seems to me to be almost less than human. He combines the ferocity of the tiger, the slyness of the fox, and the shape of a monkey. I am doubly alarmed when he is near."

"This is the natural recoil of virtue away from vice," said Jasper Very. "God has given to woman an intuitive sense which, without any long process of reasoning, shows her when a man is bad. It is her protection against his greater strength. It is the Almighty's gift to her, and is beyond the value of rubies. If she will use it, she need never be deceived as to a man's inner character."

"I suppose that is why we women can trust some people from the moment we see them and are suspicions of others from the very first."

"Undoubtedly it is; and all women should beware of men whose persons, looks, or acts repel that fine discriminating sense within them. Every man should ask himself the

Edward T. Curnick

question: 'Have I sufficient moral integrity and nobility to pass muster before the eyes of a pure-minded woman!' If he can say 'Yes' to this, he is to be congratulated."

"I am afraid most men are so self-sufficient that they think the other sex is blind to their faults, and will tolerate and cling to them whether or not."

"They may think so when they reflect only lightly; but when they consider deeply, they know that they can receive the respect of good women only when they are worthy of it. This should stimulate them to be knightly in character—pure, true, gentle, kind, brave, thoroughly good."

"I am glad you have such a high ideal, and trust you will live up to it. If so, you will be my Sir Knight, to lead me to Uncle Pete's cabin. His little girl is down with the measles, and I have promised to act as doctor and nurse for the poor child."

"I will be happy to act as your humble servant on this errand of mercy. In the meantime I wish to get your consent to go with me in a buggy to Mount Zion meeting-house next Friday. An all-day meeting is to be held there, and I am to preach in the morning. I desire the help of your voice in the singing. We can return in the afternoon. What do you say?"

"If mamma gives permission, I shall gladly go; but let us proceed now to the quarters, and you shall comfort the soul of the mother while I try to help the girl's body."

CHAPTER XV

CUPID'S CHARIOT

A one-seated buggy is Cupid's most formidable chariot. It beats an automobile farther than we can say. An automobile is an intricate piece of machinery and the driver, if he is of the right kind, will exercise the greatest care. He must look well to his steering, must diligently examine the road as he passes along to avoid obstructions, ruts and broken pieces of glass, and especially is it necessary for him to keep his car from colliding with other machines. This divides his attention and interferes very much with freedom of conversation, and that mutual joy which comes from undisturbed companionship.

As to guiding the wheel with one hand and stealing the other around the waist of a fair companion, if it were allowed by the moral law, it is prohibited by state regulation. The procedure is often dangerous in more senses than one.

But riding in a buggy is different. There is just enough attention required in driving to relieve awkwardness. If a country bumpkin is seated by his best girl, and can speak only in monosyllables, and those few and far between, he can at least say to his horse: "Git ep." If his hands are so big, red and rough that he is ashamed of them, they can by

Edward T. Curnick

holding reins and whip pass muster. His cowhide boots, shining with bear's grease or lard, can be hidden under the buggy robe.

When a young man takes the young lady of his choice for a drive, he feels a sort of proprietorship in her. He has her company all to himself. With this sensation comes another of responsibility. He must protect her from all harm and look well to her comfort. He wraps her up carefully in the thick robe, which he bought last week at the county seat, paying a half month's wages for it. He shields her from the least cold, when perhaps that very morning she has hung out a wash in her mother's yard with the temperature about zero.

When Friday morning came round Jasper Very came with it. He drove his faithful Bob, hitched to a new buggy, in front of Judge LeMonde's imposing mansion.

Presently Viola appeared, her outside wrap being a heavy beaver cloak which buttoned under her chin and reached nearly to the ground. Upon her head she wore a hat corresponding in color with her cloak. The somber hue of the hat was relieved only by a band and knot of blue ribbon; for in those days feathers and flowers were not allowed. However, she needed no outside ornament to increase her beauty. Her cheeks were red as roses as they were touched by the sharp wintry air; her eyes shone bright and clear with the look of perfect health.

Jasper Very assisted her into the vehicle and jumping in himself adjusted the heavy lap robe about them both. He spoke to Bob and they were off. Nora, the servant, with a laugh called after them: "How nice yo' look riding togedder. 'Pears like yo' made fo' each odder." Viola shook her hand at the girl, but did not seem much displeased. They went down a private way to the big gate opening on the county road and, soon striking the river road, turned to the left in an opposite direction from that which Larkin and Grimes had taken.

For a while they were a bit embarrassed, for this was the first time they had ridden in a buggy together. They confined their remarks to the weather, the bad roads, the Casey old maids (whose house they passed), the swollen Cumberland River, and other small talk. However, this constraint soon passed and they began chatting and laughing in a natural and pleasant way.

"Mr. Very," said Viola, "I want you to tell me about the adventure you had on a ferry boat, to which John Larkin referred the last time I saw him."

"That was one of the strangest experiences of my life," replied Jasper. "A couple of years ago, before coming to this region, some of my friends wanted me to run for the office of representative to the State Legislature. I did not much like the idea of ministers being put forward for political office; but, thinking if elected I might do some good at Frankfort, I consented to be a candidate. One day on my electioneering tour I was wanting to cross the river on a ferryboat, and was passing through some underbrush and woods near the embarking place when I heard some one say: 'That Jasper Very is a great rascal and so are all his preacher friends. They will steal horses and do other mean things. It is a scandal to the county that such a man as Very should be put up to run for office and the first time I see him I intend to whip him for his impudence.' This surprised me a little, and I tried to find another way of reaching the boat without passing these men; but the underbrush was so thick I had to go that way. I summoned up all my courage and rode up. There were six men talking together. I said: 'Gentlemen, who is the man among you who is going to whip Very the first time he sees him?' The man who had made the threat spoke

Edward T. Curnick

out and said: 'I am the lark that's going to thrash him well.' Said I: 'Very is known to be much of a man, and it will take a man to whip him, mind you.' 'O no,' said he, 'I can whip any such preacher the Lord ever made!' 'Well, sir,' said I, 'you cannot do it. My name is Very and, as I never like to live in dread, if you really intend to whip me, come and do it now.' He looked confused, and said: 'Oh, you can't fool me that way. You are not Very.' 'Well,' said I, 'that is my name, and now is your time. If you must whip me do it now.' He said: 'No, no, you are not Very at all; you only want to fool me.' By this time we had got into the boat and he began again cursing Very. I said to a gentleman: 'Please hold my horse,' and stepping up to the cursing disciple said sternly to him: 'Now sir, you have to whip me as you threatened or quit cursing me, or I will put you in the river and baptize you in the name of the devil, for you surely belong to him.' This settled him and, strange to say, when election day came he voted for me, and has been my friend ever since."

"I am glad he learned such a needed and salutary lesson," said Viola. "I have heard my father say that a braggart is generally a coward. My mind commends your course, Mr. Very, of walking boldly up to danger and daring it to do its worst; but my woman's heart shrinks from the presence of peril."

"Merely to think upon danger makes you and most women timid; but when the reality comes I believe your sex is as brave as mine. In many encounters with rough and wicked men in the wilderness I have found that a bold front is the best way to avoid evils which threaten. A brave word, backed by a good cause, often disarms an adversary."

Thus with anecdote, comment, and talk of church work they rode along, their acquaintanceship increasing, and each, scarcely conscious of the act, looking into each other's heart to find there its thoughts and feelings.

When they had approached within a half mile of Shiloh meeting house, their destination, Jasper said: "Miss Viola, you remember I requested you to sing at this coming service. Perhaps you expected to join your voice only with that of the congregation, but I want you to favor us with a solo before I rise to preach. It will be something new at Shiloh, but all the more impressive for that. The other evening I heard you sing in your drawing-room that inspiring hymn:

'Lo! he comes with clouds descending,
Once for favored sinners slain.'

"Now I am to preach this morning on 'Christ's Second Coming,' and the hymn will be a good introduction to the sermon. Will you agree to sing it?"

He looked down into her eyes to see if he could find consent in them. She did not answer immediately, but seemed to be in deep thought. Finally she looked up into his face, and there was a trace of tears in her blue eyes as she said: "Mr. Very, I have never stood alone before the public and sung. It would be a great trial for me to do so today; but if by singing I can glorify my Master by helping some poor soul to a better life, and if I can be of any aid to you, I will do the best I can."

"Thank you, Viola (somehow he forgot to use the 'Miss'), and I am sure God's Holy Spirit will use your voice to benefit many this day."

Soon they reached Shiloh meeting house, and were welcomed by John Larkin and Nathaniel Grimes who had finished their meeting at Bridgewater and had come to this all-day gathering. In fact, Larkin was in charge of it.

Edward T. Curnick

As usual, on such occasions many horses were hitched to trees and saplings, a large number of the people having come long distances.

At ten o'clock the great service of the morning began. The church was filled with an expectant crowd, for it was generally known that Jasper Very was to preach. Jasper and several other ministers were seated on a long bench back of the pulpit. The preliminary exercises were over and all were looking for the speaker to begin his sermon, when Jasper Very arose and quietly said: "Friends, Miss Viola LeMonde has kindly consented to sing a solo at this time." Many eyes were at once turned to the young lady, who was sitting to the right of the pulpit. Her beautiful face flushed a little with their scrutiny; but she at once arose and walking in front of the wooden table which answered for a pulpit, without any help from organ or piano (the room having no such instrument) she began singing that stirring hymn:

"Lo! he comes with clouds descending."

As she proceeded with the song all timidity left her and she became possessed with the sentiment of the piece. When she sang

"Every eye shall now behold him
Clothed in glorious majesty,"

she raised her own eyes toward heaven, as though she saw the Son of man seated at the right hand of God's throne. A feeling of awe mingled with joy seized the people, and they also looked upward, drawn by the rapt gaze of the singer.

Her face looked like that of an angel as, transported with her theme, she sang in a pure soprano voice:

"Yea, amen! let all adore thee,
High on thy eternal throne;
Savior, take the power and glory,
Claim the kingdom for thine own:
Jah! Jehovah!
Everlasting God, come down."

As she called upon the God of heaven to descend upon that company she lifted her hand toward the low and humble roof, and with her eyes still gazing up she seemed to see the Son of man coming in his glory on the clouds of power. The effect was marvellous. Many people were in tears. Some sighed deeply as though for relief while others, raising their arms above their heads, shouted the praises of God.

When Viola took her seat Jasper Very arose in his place and stood looking over his congregation for some moments in silence. He did not wish to destroy the effects of the song— and wanted to give the people time to quiet their aroused feelings. He then proceeded with his discourse on our Lord's second appearing, but though he preached in his usual masterly way and held the attention of his audience throughout the tide of feeling did not rise as high as when Viola sang. He was willing that she should bear the honors of the occasion. That singing was long remembered and passed into tradition among the people.

Edward T. Curnick

CHAPTER XVI

HORSE THIEVES

Springtime in Kentucky. One wants a new language to express its charms. Winter's shadows fly away. Clouds that looked dark, heavy, and threatening are followed by rosy sunsets and luminous peaks in the sky which appear like mountains standing round about the New Jerusalem. A warm breath of nature starts from the spicy islands south of the great Gulf, crosses it, then sweeps along Mississippi's mighty valley to the "happy hunting ground," bearing in its soft embrace birds of many wing—robin, bluebird, thrush, and sparrow. This breath melts the icy fetters of the streams, and they sing a sweet song of welcome. It enfolds the trees, and they put forth millions of little green ears to hear what the streams are saying. It fondly caresses the flower bushes, and they swell almost to bursting with reviving beauty. Like the green bush which Moses saw aflame with holy fire, every branch and twig shows the mystic presence of nature's God.

While birds with brightened plumage sing as though their lives would escape through their throats; while lambs, calves, and colts gambol in the pasture, filled with the happiness of young life; while fish rush upstream like flashes of silver light and the very trees clap their hands in praise, it is not conceivable that man, God's masterpiece, should be insensible to this season of the year. A sudden thrill like an electric current passes through his being; a subtle exhilaration, as when a man is filled with wine, possesses him, and he is in touch with the new life, whether he goes afield with team or plow or hunts the forest for the increasing game.

It was a day in early April. All the planters were busy in their fields, either laboring with their own hands or superintending the toil of their slaves. The negroes—those jocund children of nature—with happy faces and plantation melodies on their lips, were preparing the ground for its grain and tobacco seed. Judge LeMonde himself was in a rich field between his house and the river giving directions to his chief overseer. In the front garden, between the house and pine trees, could be seen Madam and Viola LeMonde and Mose and Nora all busy putting flower beds in order. Mose was digging the ground, Nora was using a light rake, and the white women were putting in some flower seeds.

While such peaceful work was being done in the river bottom, another scene was taking place at Simon Wiles' hillside farm. Though the season and weather called to earnest effort, we see Sam Wiles and Zibe Turner, the monster dwarf, seated on a big log behind the barn. Let us listen to what they are saying:

Wiles: "De ol' Jedge guv us a term in de jug (jail), an' I'm sure goin' to git even wuth him an' dat preacher too."

Turner: "I'll be wuth you in ary scrape you want to git up, but we uns must be keerful not to be ketched ag'in."

Wiles: "Cordin' to my thinkin', each month we'uns war in de jug is wurth de price of a hoss."

Turner: "That's yer game, is it? Well, 'tain't de fust time we'uns hev borrowed a hoss an' fergot to return 'im, but we'uns never struck so high up as de Jedge's stock. What hosses air you thinkin' on?"

Wiles: "What ones do you suppose? De best ones, o' course. We'uns must take Velox for de money he will bring in Paducky, an' I want to bring down de pride o' dat young upstart, George LeMonde. We'uns both owed 'im a grudge sence he beat you in de race an' won what leetle money we'uns had. De nex' best hoss in de barn is Dolly, an' we'll take her 'long to keep de bay compney."

Turner: "Dat suits me all right; but I want to ride Velox, 'cause he went past me in de race. Won't I make 'im trabble, do, down de ribber road! Dat's my holt."

Wiles: "We'uns must wait till we git a good night. De moon is full now, an' de light is too bright. Four nights from now it will rise purty late, an' den we'll proceed to bizness. We'uns want a leetle light to show us how to git in de bawn an' move 'round. I hear dad callin' me to go plowin', so we'uns must be goin'. Dis is Friday. Come to de house tomorrer evenin', an' we'uns'll settle de partic'lars."

The two men parted, Sam Wiles to help his father to prepare to plant their small crop of corn, wheat and tobacco, and Zibe Turner, with the cunning of a fox and the look of a savage bear, to slink through the backwoods to his mother's little cabin some miles distant.

Monday night was a time just suited to their designs. They had to act very cautiously for horse stealing at that time in Kentucky was considered almost the greatest crime in the catalogue, and woe betide any horse thief who was caught and found guilty! There was little danger of the "law's delay" in his case, for a rope and a limb of a tree prevented all court expenses.

By a small bridge near Franklin Schoolhouse Sam Wiles met by appointment Zibe Turner and the two walked along the road, having little fear of being seen as it was near midnight. They soon reached Judge LeMonde's barn lot and now had to use the utmost caution not to arouse the great dog Sport or any of his satellites. By degrees they pushed open the heavy gate. Then they went to the barn door through which the horses were led to their stalls. It was fastened, but with a common lock. Wiles had brought a bunch of keys for just such an emergency, and after trying two or three found one which fitted the lock. In a moment they were inside the great barn. A long row of stalls was just before them. They carefully closed the door and Wiles, taking a flint and steel and some tinder from his pocket, struck out a spark which ignited the tinder. He then applied a long brimstone match to the tinder, and at once the match was ablaze. They soon found in which stalls were the horses they wanted, Velox being in the first stall and Dolly in the third. Back of the horses were pegs upon which hung harnesses. Wiles quickly unbuckled Dolly's halter and put a riding bridle on her. He then selected a fine saddle and placed it upon her back. Turner did the same for Velox. They then reopened the barn door, and Turner led Velox into the yard. Wiles at once followed with Dolly. To prevent all suspicion they closed the barn door but left it unlocked. It seemed as though they would get away without arousing man or dog; but just as they were leading the horses through the barn gate Velox, perhaps incensed at being taken from his stall at that unseemly hour and leaving his mates, gave a loud neigh.

This sound was heard by Sport who was sleeping in a coach house at the rear of the mansion six hundred feet away. At once the faithful animal, suspecting something was wrong,

Edward T. Curnick

set up a great barking, and was instantly joined by a group of dogs which were with him. The thieves, being afraid that the barking would arouse the plantation, jumped into their saddles and rode quietly along the county road till they reached the river road a quarter of a mile beyond. Here they stopped to observe if anything would happen at the house.

Now the acute ears of the dogs had heard the hoofbeats of the horses in the still night, and they continued to emit a chorus of barks. At last their noise awoke Judge LeMonde, who was dreaming that twenty lawyers were all pleading a case at once. Thinking something unusual was the matter, he arose and dressed and called up George, his son. Together they went out to the carriage house and tried to quiet the dogs, but they continued barking. The men could find nothing out of place. But the judge, being somewhat uneasy, said to his son: "Let us go down to the barn and see whether or not the horses are all right."

So they started down the road, past the negro cabins (all the slaves being sound asleep), and on to the barn. They went into the barn, and soon discovered the absence of the horses. The judge was a man of decision and courage. He said: "George, thieves have broken into the barn and stolen our two best horses. I do not believe they have been gone long. Run instantly and arouse Mose and some of the other slaves. Tell your mother what has happened, and say that we are going at once to follow the thieves. While you are gone I will get out Prince, Clay and Bess, and we will go after the villains."

George ran to do his father's bidding, and soon most of the whites and slaves on the place were informed of the theft, and were wild with excitement as a result.

In the meantime Wiles and Turner saw the lights in the house and were sure their deed was discovered. It was too late to return the horses to the barn, and they decided to carry out their first intention and ride them as rapidly as possible twenty-five miles down the river road, and there deliver them to a confederate, who would smuggle them to a horse dealer in Paducah. They put spurs to their horses and the noble brutes started down the river road at a fast gait. At the beginning the thieves had every advantage. They were mounted upon Judge LeMonde's fastest horses, and they had several minutes' start of their pursuers. So that they were more than a mile down the river road when the chase began.

"Ha! Ha!" laughed Zibe Turner, "I 'spects I'm ahead in dis race. De time befo' Velox passed me; but now I'm ridin' him, an' I'd like to see de debil hisself overtake me."

"We'uns air safe," said Wiles, "but we'uns must hold back our hosses sum, for we uns hev a good jaunt to take, an' it won't do to tire 'em out at fust."

Both acted at once on this sensible advice, and they brought the ready animals down to a moderate trot. It was now a little past midnight, and not a soul was to be seen on the road. A light breeze blew softly from the south, shaking the tiny forest leaves and blowing across the fields to welcome the coming footsteps of another day.

Though these bad men boasted to each other that they had the winning hand, there was some uneasiness in their hearts. They knew that this was the highest stake they had ever played; they were striking at the chief man of the county, and had stolen the best horses on his plantation. Should the heavy hand of justice smite them, it would be a stunning blow. The voice of conscience was not utterly dead, and it aroused fears in their hearts that they were not willing to acknowledge even to themselves; but, like many other desperate men, their

Edward T. Curnick

very alarm occasioned a fiercer determination to show a bold front.

About two o'clock that morning honest David Hester, who lived about fifteen miles distant from Judge LeMonde, was awakened from his deep sleep by a pounding in his barn, which stood not far from his house. Honest David knew at once what was the matter,—his horse Jim was kicking in his stall. This valuable beast had a habit at irregular intervals of kicking and pawing in the barn. Once or twice his restless feeling had made him use his legs so vigorously that he was thrown in his stall; and if his owner had not come to his help, he might have been fatally hurt. This night Jim's knocking was specially violent. Farmer Hester at last arose and went to the barn to quiet the restless creature. Speaking kindly to him, he turned him into a box stall and returned to the house.

Just as he was entering the rear door he heard the sound of horses' hoofs some distance up the river road. His curiosity aroused, he decided to see who the early travelers were. He walked to the front yard and stood under a large lilac bush which was already covered thickly with leaves.

The horsemen came on quickly. The moonlight was not sufficiently clear for David to see distinctly; but he noticed that the rider nearer him was a short man mounted on a dark horse, and that the other was a larger man riding a lighter-colored horse having a white spot in its forehead. David did not recognize either the men or horses, but the suspicion flashed across his mind that the lighter-colored horse was Judge LeMonde's Dolly. However, he was not sure, and in a moment the men had ridden by.

Honest David returned to his house and bed. It proved, however, to be a night of interruptions, for he had hardly gotten between the sheets and fallen into a sound slumber before there came a loud knocking at the front door. David—and in fact his whole household—was aroused thereby, and hastening to the window, he tried to learn what was the matter. He saw in the yard below three men standing by three horses and heard the quick and eager words of Judge LeMonde: "Hurry, Friend David, and come to our help. My barn was broken into about midnight and my horses Velox and Dolly stolen from it. We are almost sure the thieves headed this way down the river, for where the county road meets the river road we examined the hoofprints as best we could, and decided the horses turned this way."

"Yes, Judge, I'll help you all I can, and will be down in a hurry." Honest Hester left the window and was soon down in the yard, followed presently by his sons, wife and daughter Henrietta, all greatly excited by the news.

Judge LeMonde continued: "We three have ridden our horses very hard, and cannot hope to overtake the thieves without fresh animals. They were careful to take my best blooded stock, and had considerable start of us. Will you kindly favor us with the loan of some of your horses? With them I think we may overtake the rascals."

"That I will, Judge," said Hester, "and my boys and I will go along to help capture the rogues. I am sure you are on the right track, for half an hour ago I saw two men riding past on horseback, and I suspicioned one horse was your Dolly, for it had a white star in its forehead, but I was not dead sure."

The men now hurried to the barn, and Jim was taken out to do something besides pawing in his stall. Other horses were brought out and soon seven men vaulted into saddles,—Judge LeMonde, his son George, his servant Mose, David Hester and three of his stalwart sons. One son remained behind to care for the three horses, which were covered with mud, foam, sweat, and were badly winded.

Though in such haste, Judge LeMonde could not forget his duty to the ladies. He apologized for so rudely disturbing their slumbers, and thanked them for their interest and sympathy in his undertaking. They lifted their hats and were away down the road. Madam Hester and her daughter waved them adieu, watching the riders as far as they could in the dim light.

As they were passing through the hamlet of Bridgewater Mose saluted his master by lifting his hand to his wooly head (in the hurry of starting he had not thought of his hat), and said: "Mas'r LeMonde. I 'spect we mus' ride like de win' in dis stretch ob de race; fer I had hearn der is a byroad ten miles furder on which leads inter a mighty wild place wid many windin' paths; an' ef de tiefs gets dar, dey'll sho' give us de slip."

David Hester, having traveled this road before, corroborated the negro's words.

Judge LeMonde replied: "The advice Mose gives is very good, so we must travel with utmost speed, for we must make every effort to capture the scoundrels."

With this they all gave rein to their horses and made rapid progress down the road. The men were so intent on watching the road and guiding their horses that few words were spoken as they went along.

Those who are acquainted with the river road below Bridgewater will remember that the knobs come very near to the river and the road runs close to the foot of the hills. Hence there is not much chance for a horseman to escape from his pursuers except by outriding them.

Sam Wiles and Zibe Turner had come within three miles of the place of which Mose had spoken. They were congratulating themselves on their good fortune, when the quick ears of Turner heard the sounds of horses' hoofs some distance in the rear. "Pard," he said, "hear dat? Da air on our track, sure as shootin', an' by de sound I know der is sev'ral on 'em."

"What can we do?" asked Wiles. "De knobs air too steep to climb, for der ain't no roads about here, an' de ribber is near us on de left. Our only chance is to reach de forks of de road 'fore dey can overtake us. But Dolly is purty well played out. Der ain't much go in her. How is Velox standin' it?"

"My hoss shows his blood an' trainin'," said Turner. "He's all in a sweat an' lather an' he breathes fast, but I tink he's good for de distance. You'uns must gib Dolly mo' whip and spur. Better to kill her dan to be tuk."

Wiles thought the monster dwarf's words sensible, and he drove the cruel spurs into poor Dolly's sides without mercy and lashed her with the whip. The gallant mare responded with increased speed. But it was like the flicker of a candle almost consumed.

Just at this time, the morning now beginning to break, the thieves were discovered by their pursuers, who, thus encouraged, sent up a shout together and urged their horses to greater speed. The animals, still comparatively fresh, increased their gait and gained rapidly upon those ahead. It was now a desperate race. Horseflesh was not considered by either party,—only a wild desire to escape by one and a determination to bring the outlaws to justice by the other.

Strange to say, the dwarf became the leader in this terrible emergency, perhaps because he felt there was yet considerable reserve power in his mount, Velox. "Hang to her a

Edward T. Curnick

leetle longer, Sam," he cried. "One quarter mile mo', an' we can shake 'em off. Speak to Dolly, gib her her head, an' spur her in a fresh place."

This Wiles did. "Go it, Dolly! Good girl! Show 'em your heels! A few rods mo'."

But it was no use. The limit of her strength was reached. Her breath came in gasps, her flanks trembled, she began staggering as she ran, and when within a hundred feet of the turn she fell head foremost, throwing her rider to the ground and falling heavily on her side.

Even in this predicament the monster dwarf did not lose his nerve; he halted Velox a second and said to his chief: "I'll git away on Velox an' cum to yer help ef I can. Keep a stiff upper lip. Nevah say die. Dat's my holt. Good-by."

With this he again drove the spurs into Velox's side, and was off. It was time, for his pursuers were shouting, "Halt! Halt!" and then the sharp crack of rifles was heard, and balls went whizzing by Turner's head. But he was soon at the turn, and with one wild yell of mingled triumph and hate he turned to the right, plunged into the thick woods, and was lost to sight. He had escaped.

In the meantime Sam Wiles, half dazed by his fall, was still lying on the ground when the Judge and his men rode up. Quickly the Judge said to Hester: "You hold Wiles and I will attend to Dolly."

They all dismounted and Hester did as requested. The Judge, George, and Mose drew near to faithful Dolly, and the Judge knelt down and took her head in his lap and spoke to her in soothing tones. He asked for water for her and George ran for some, but it was too late. Her eyes were already becoming glazed in death; but she gazed up into her owner's face with a look of recognition. Then a shiver went through her frame, she closed her eyes, and ceased to breathe.

The Judge and George wept, and were not ashamed to show their tears; while Mose, who had always cared for the horse, sobbed aloud in his grief, and on a sudden impulse of anger administered a kick to prostrate Wiles, the "po' white trash," who had killed Mas'r's hoss.

Judge LeMonde gave directions for Mose to bury Dolly's body in a decent manner, and then the rest prepared to return to their homes.

CHAPTER XVII

LYNCH LAW OR THE GOSPEL

Wiles, the captive horse thief, was given Mose's horse to ride and, closely guarded by the six men, they all retraced their journey up the river road. Wiles was sullen and morose, having little to say. His look was that of a guilty and disappointed man, yet he carried a don't care, half defiant air which was more assumed than real.

Bad news travels fast. The very atmosphere seems to tear it from house to house. Farmers had begun to pass along the road in their wagons; they heard and spread the account of the horse-stealing. It flashed through the hamlet of Bridgewater with incredible rapidity. As men heard the reports they became wildly excited and grimly determined to punish the thieves if caught. Some, by nature more excitable than others, left their work and rode down the road to aid as best they could in the pursuit. These met the party as it was returning, and swelled their number. They were not backward in expressing their opinions of the culprit as they cast black and angry looks upon him.

These people of the "bottoms" were of a higher class than the "poor whites" who abode in the hills. They lived in far better houses, they had better school and church privileges, and their sense of moral values was keener than the others. While as a rule they were not experts in grammar and rhetoric, their language was much superior to that heard in the back districts.

"Lynch him," "Fill his carcass with bullets," "String him up high as Haman," "He's been in many scrapes like this; now we've caught him, let's make short work of him," "Hanging is too good for him; he ought to be skinned alive,"—such were some of the expressions which saluted Wiles' ears, and they did not serve to make his nerves any more quiet.

When the men reached Bridgewater the morning was well advanced and they were met by a considerable company from the village and surrounding plantations. There were a few women among the crowd and a few children. Any one looking upon that gathering could see that they threatened vengeance. Hiram Sanders, the herculean blacksmith, was their leader. This was the blacksmith who was a terror to all wrestlers, and who was never whipped except once, and then by Jasper Very. When Jasper came into those parts Sanders said: "I've licked all the preachers who have come around here and I intend to lick this one." The two met on horseback, dismounted, and began their bout. The blacksmith had found his match and Very with a desperate effort threw the fellow over an adjoining fence. Sanders' pride and fighting spirit were both broken, and he humbly said: "If you please, Mr. Preacher, will you be so kind as to throw my horse over the fence too?" His defeat put Sanders on good terms with Very and now they were close friends.

As the men guarding Wiles entered Bridgewater they were met and stopped by the crowd which had gathered. The mighty blacksmith walked up to Judge LeMonde and, addressing him in a respectful manner said: "Judge, we have heard about this bad scrape; but we want to know the straight

Edward T. Curnick

of it, and you will obleege us by telling it from first to last!"

Judge LeMonde stated the facts in a clear and simple manner. As he proceeded with his account the feelings of the crowd became more and more aroused; and when he closed with a description of Dolly's death a general cry of denunciation was raised.

Then up spoke Sanders to the people: "Friends and feller citizens, this is a case which needs keerful thought and treatment. It is a case which only men should decide, and I ask that all the women and children go back home and all the men of this company adjourn to the bridge over Honey Crick near by, that we can quietly give this matter all the attention it requires."

His request was heeded and soon some thirty or forty men were on the bridge, with Wiles seated on a log which had been placed in the middle of the structure. The men disposed themselves in any way they saw fit, some leaning against the bridge railing, others sitting on the floor with their legs hanging over the water, and others bringing logs or sticks upon which to sit.

As this was likely to be mob law Sanders, and not Judge LeMonde, was elected chairman and the deliberations commenced at once. Sanders said: "Men, what have you got to say ag'inst the prisoner! Let any one speak that wants to."

William Hester, honest David Hester's oldest son, was the first to respond: "We on the river bottom have endured this Wiles crowd a good while. We know they are a curse to this section. They steal our hosses and whatever they can lay their hands on. They make 'licit whisky in the hills and knobs. They are lazy and shiftless, and no count in general. They scare our women, and are a nuisance and pest all around. I say we oughter make an example of Wiles, the ringleader of the gang, and put him out of the way of killing any more hosses by making him stretch a rope from this bridge."

"You have listened to what Bill Hester has said. Has any other gentleman any remarks to make?" asked their chairman.

Abner Hunt, a fiery little man, whose plantation joined that of David Hester, spoke in rapid tones, emphasizing his words with vigorous gesticulations: "I fully agree with what Bill has said. Most all the people living on these here bottoms are peaceable and law-abiding and it is too bad that a few desprit villians should keep the county in a state of terror and alarm. If there were some big rattle snakes in our midst, we would try to ketch and kill them; and these human rascals are worse than rattlers. My vote is to string him up quick."

"We want a free and full discussion of this case, and I wait to hear any one else speak," said Sanders.

Then Hans Schmidt, a large, fair-faced German, arose, and said: "Mine freunds, dis ist a wery serious matter, und we must consider it with much deliberation. Gott's Book tells us to luv our enemies, und we should not show hate und refenge to any man. We all know Wiles is vun great rogue, und I would give much money to see heem out of the bottom; but I would not like to haf a hand in lynching heem. I tink it is better for the law to take its course and for us to deliver heem up to prison."

These words acted like sparks to gunpowder, and several in the crowd cried: "No! No!" "Hang him!" "Don't let him escape!" A few others said they agreed with what Schmidt had proposed.

Edward T. Curnick

When quiet was restored, one more speaker was heard. His name was Damon Craig. He was a hill farmer who made a good living for himself and family by industry and economy on the thin soil above the river bottom. All highly respected him and his words had much weight: "Thur is al'ys danger in takin; a hoss thief to jail. Dey air slick by natur' and der bizness makes 'em slicker. You'uns can't trust sich a feller as Wiles ur Turner a minit. Ef you'uns put 'im in jail he mought 'scape, and aryhow we don't know but sum smart lawyers might cl'ar 'im ur git a light sentence for 'im. So I'm in favor uv riddin' de kentry uv 'im right now, and I'll be de fust to pull de rope."

This speech was received by nods of assent and cries of "Good!" "Good!" "That's the talk!" by many in the crowd.

After Craig had spoken Sanders looked at Judge LeMonde and thus addressed him: "Judge, you are the most interested person in this company. You have lost two fine hosses and been put to the most trouble. It is only right that we should hear from you before we take a vote. Would you like to say anything?"

Upon this invitation Judge LeMonde arose from the log upon which he was sitting. His clothing was bespattered with mud and his face showed the struggle both physical and mental through which he had passed. But even with these limitations he appeared the typical judge. A serious but composed look was in his eyes. It was with deep feeling that he addressed the group of determined men.

"Neighbors and friends," said he, "many of you I have known from my youth, and I am glad to call you friends. I wish to thank you for the interest you have shown in my welfare by aiding me in every possible way to regain my stolen property; and while my good Velox is now far away from me, probably never to return, and my noble Dolly is buried by the roadside, you have helped to capture the chief criminal in the affair. I do not wonder that this dastardly act has stung you to the quick and that your honest hearts cry out for justice to be visited upon the guilty. But you will pardon me if I differ from most of you as to how that justice should be administered. Let us remember that the sovereign State of Kentucky has laws upon her statute books meting out just punishment for all crimes. She has suitable machinery for the execution of those laws—courts, judges, lawyers, police, jails, penitentiary—and it is the duty of all citizens to abide by the laws they have made. Therefore I cannot agree with your arguments nor justify your wish to take the law into your own hands. My voice is, let the miserable culprit be taken to the county jail, be tried before the court and receive his punishment in a lawful manner."

Judge LeMonde's speech made a visible impression on the men and possibly his advice would have been heeded had not Sanders, the chairman, spoken. These were his words: "With all respect to the Judge's remarks I think his premises are wrong. We have an unwritten law in Kentucky that hoss thieves should be put out of the world as soon as they are caught and proved guilty. It saves time, danger of escape, and expense to the State. This is a clear case for Wiles was caught in the very act, and we are quite sure this is not his first offense. My opinion is the county should be rid of such trash, and the sooner the better. We will now vote on the case. All in favor of hanging Sam Wiles at this time for hoss stealing raise your hands." Thirty hands were lifted up. "All opposed raise your hands." Five put up their hands and a few refused to vote.

In spite of protests made by Judge LeMonde and others, preparations for the tragic act were quickly made. A man had cut a clothesline in his yard and had brought it to the bridge.

Edward T. Curnick

Hiram Sanders spoke quickly and with a tone of authority: "Damon Craig, take this rope, tie a small stone to one end, and throw it over that big limb of the tall walnut tree standing by the crick."

Damon Craig instantly obeyed, and with one attempt the rope was thrown over and both ends were near the ground. It was the work of only a minute or two to bring the miserable prisoner under the limb and to adjust the rope in the form of a hangman's knot around his neck.

When this was done Sanders said: "Wiles, we don't want to send you out of this world without giving you a chance for preparation; so if you want to pray or to send any message to your dad or mam, we'll wait for you."

Wiles was a man not without physical courage, and in this trying hour his grit did not fail him. He cast one hurried glance around, as though looking for some allies to aid him, but none were in sight. He gazed into the faces of those standing near him to see if there were any relenting; but the stern and determined looks of most of these men showed him it was useless to expect mercy from them. All hope seemed gone. Wiles, apparently wishing more to show a brave front to man than a humble and contrite spirit to God, simply said: "I've nuthin' to say to de likes uv you'uns; only I defy ye to do yer wu'st."

"Haul away!" cried Sanders, and a dozen men seizing the rope, began pulling it, tightening the noose around Wiles' neck; but before they had lifted the body free from the ground a loud beating of horses' hoofs was heard in the direction of Bridgewater. Instinctively the men ceased from their work to look down the road. Perhaps there was a tremor of fear and condemnation in their hearts. We believe that every man who purposes in his heart to help lynch one of his fellow men, if he allows reason and conscience half a chance to be heard, will not engage in the attempt.

Presently two men came in sight, riding as though their lives depended upon their haste. They were Jasper Very and John Larkin, who had heard of the proposed lynching. The riders spurred their horses across the bridge and flung themselves from their saddles, but not before Jasper Very had shouted in his loudest voice: "Men, I call upon you in the name of God to stop this wicked act." Then, rushing up to the condemned man, who was already gasping for breath, he pulled the rope from over the limb sufficiently to loosen the knot around Wiles' neck. The lynchers were too much surprised to resist.

While John Larkin held the weakened prisoner Jasper Very removed the rope from his neck, and the two preachers helped Wiles to a seat on the bridge. Here Very stood over him as though he were his guardian angel. His eyes blazed with a fire never seen in them before. His gigantic form seemed to swell to larger proportions. He looked the incarnation of power tempered with pity. Very spoke with his heart hot within him: "Men of Kentucky, I am ashamed of your actions this day. What you purpose doing is a stain upon our State. It is a crime the memory of which, if committed, you will not be able to hide from your minds till life's last hour. Do you not know that two sins can never make an act right? How do you dare to hurry this man into the presence of his Maker unprepared? How can you meet such a sin at the judgment day? There are the courts. Let Sam Wiles be tried in them. You are well aware that our laws are very severe against horse-stealing, and when brought to the bar of justice the prisoner will suffer the full penalty of his deeds. But there is a higher law than those in our criminal courts. It is God's law, given to the children of men amid the thunders of Mount Sinai when the whole mountain was black with a thick cloud of smoke, which

Edward T. Curnick

rolled away as from a great furnace into the sky. God descended in fire upon the mount. Thunders roared, lightnings flashed, and the peaks trembled to their foundations. The trumpets sounded louder and louder and the awful voice of almighty God 'shook the earth.' What were the commandments there given? One of them was: 'Thou shalt not kill.' Do not think that lynch law is not murder. It is murder of a very deplorable kind; for the perpetrators of the deed are not one but many, so that many are guilty of shedding their brother's blood. In the name of Him whose I am and whom I serve as a humble ambassador, I call upon you to desist from this proposed crime, conceived in passion and carried forward under great excitement. Listen to the voice of reason, and your consciences will approve your course."

What the majesty of the law could not do under the words of the honored Judge, the power of the gospel accomplished through the agency of the backwoods preacher.

Hiram Sanders was the first to yield. "Neighbors," he said, "what the preacher spoke is true. I think we will sleep sounder tonight if we spare the prisoner, though he is a sneaking, onery critter. But let the law take its course. We must see that he is securely guarded and lodged in jail without a mishap."

Under a strong guard Wiles was taken up the river road to be placed in the county jail. The planters and others returned to their usual work, while Judge LeMonde and his company rode home at their leisure.

CHAPTER XVIII

APPLE BLOSSOMS

May Day had come in Kentucky, and all the air was sweet with the odor of blossoms. Jasper Very had made an afternoon call at Judge LeMonde's mansion; and the day being so charming he had invited Miss Viola to walk with him to the apple orchard which was in full bloom. The two walked down the gentle hill on which the house was built and proceeded along a private road leading north toward the knob. They passed by tilled fields in which green things were peeping through the soil. They skirted a pasture where horses and cows were grazing in perfect content. Then they went through a wide gateway and at once came into the apple orchard.

The apple blossom was Jasper's favorite flower. He thought an apple tree in bloom was the nearest approach to Eden's tree of life of any sight on earth. And to behold scores of these trees filled him with such strange, happy feelings that it was difficult for him to control his emotions.

As they walked up the gradual slope which was the beginning of the swell of the knob they gazed upon many trees so thick with blossoms that they looked like gigantic bouquets. Under one of these trees they sat down upon a

Edward T. Curnick

rustic seat and looked upon the myriads of blossoms above and around them. The mystic scene—radiant sunshine, smiling landscape, balmy, odorous air, humming of bees, and pyramids of apple blossoms—increased the preacher's rapturous love of nature, God's revelation of his glory, and by a reasonable transition his heart beat with a warm, tender, and holy affection for the beautiful girl at his side. Her mind also was open to the beauties of the scene, and a thousand voices were calling her to sip the magic waters of love. She removed her broad hat and, letting it fall by her side, held it there with careless grace by one of its strings. Her golden hair added an exquisite touch to the picture.

Jasper was the first to speak: "Miss Viola, what is so beautiful as an apple tree in bloom? Our heavenly Father seems to have mixed the elements of nature to make this blossom with a skill not seen elsewhere. It combines the pure whiteness of the plum or cherry with the delicate color of the pink or rose. How beautiful is the shading! How the pink tint improves the white and the white the pink! Every separate blossom is fit to adorn the head of a fairy; and when you look upon this wilderness of bloom, you feel that the floral world can go no farther with its gift of beauty. As I sit under this bower of loveliness I am inclined to adapt the poet's words:

'My willing soul would stay
In such a place as this,
And sit and sing herself away
To everlasting bliss.'"

"I am not surprised," said Viola, "that you are enraptured with this scene. To my mind the perfection of out-of-doors life is to be among the apple blossoms, to feast one's eyes upon their delicate colors, and to inhale their sweet odor. The Hesperides of the ancients must have had a pleasant task in guarding the golden apples which Terra gave to Juno as a wedding gift."

"Yes," remarked Jasper; "and not only has mythology used this fruit to embellish the joy and sacredness of the marriage rite, but the Holy Bible makes the apple tree a type of the lover and of love; for we read: 'As the apple tree among the trees of the wood, so is my beloved among the sons.' And, 'Comfort me with apples.' Such pictures as these suggest the purest affection. May I not say they promote love?"

Viola was not willing to give a direct answer to his question, so she artfully changed the subject, saying: "The sun will soon descend behind the forest trees, and we must leave the apple blossoms and their lessons and betake ourselves to the house."

She placed her hat upon her head and arose to go. The preacher also arose, thinking to himself: "I wish I could change the apple blossoms into orange blossoms and see them crowning her golden hair."

They had walked along the farm road, and had nearly reached the garden gate when they saw the slave Mose running rapidly toward the house. They were just ascending the hill when the black man, getting within speaking distance, cried out: "Miss Vi'la, Ah jist cum frum town, an' what do yo' 'spose? Sam Wiles hab' 'scaped frum jail. He got out las' night. Sumhow he got a file an' cut two ba's out'n his cell winder an' crep' through. In sum way he clim' ober de yawd fence an' got cl'ar 'way. De she'ff an' constables is now chasin' 'im an' callin' on all who can to help run 'im down. Ah's gwine to hurry to de house to tell Mas'r LeMonde uv de 'scape."

With this remark Mose ran on, his white eyeballs rolling in

Edward T. Curnick

his excitement and his head bobbing from one side to the other.

In a few minutes Viola and Jasper were with Judge LeMonde and the rest of the house. The Judge was questioning his faithful servant: "Did the officers think he had any help in escaping?"

"Yessar, sum one mus' 'a' sperited dat file inter de jail, an' ob cou'se no ossifer would 'a dun it."

"Who do they think was his helper?"

"Zibe Turner. Two er free in de town see 'im sneakin' roun', but befo' dey could grab 'im he war gone. He seems to be in league wif de debil, an' can become inwisible when he wants ter."

"But how could the monster dwarf get the file to him?"

"It am 'sposed he had a secret talk wif de colored cook, Dinah, an' sum way cum it ober her—bewitched her mor'n likely ur gib 'er a big lot ob money—an' she passed de file in sum ob Wiles' food, an' he cut his way out."

"But his cell was in the second story, and how did he reach the ground?"

"He made a rope ob de bedclothes an' clum down dem. Dey thinks he frew de same rope ober de wall, an' Turner held de outer end while Wiles clum to de top; den he could easy drap to de bottom. Ah 'spects dey bof cl'ar out togedder, an' by dis time air way back on de knobs safe an' sound."

Judge LeMonde said: "We must do all we can to recapture Wiles and arrest Turner, for they are desperate men, and will stop at nothing to secure their own ends. However, I am afraid it will be almost impossible to take them if they have reached the fastnesses of the hills. They can hide in caves, ravines, and forests, and, being so well acquainted with the region, they can well-nigh defy pursuit."

The Judge's opinion was sound; for after the officers and citizens had hunted them for days with the aid of blood-hounds, and found them not, the effort was abandoned.

CHAPTER XIX

A PROPOSAL WITHOUT WORDS

It was on a Tuesday afternoon in the latter part of June when a note was presented to Jasper Very by a farmer living near his boarding place who had been quite a distance up river.

The note read as follows:

Silver Springs Camp Ground, June 23, 18—.

The Rev. Jasper Very,

Dear Mr. Very:—The Silver Springs Camp Meeting which began a few days ago is having fine success. It is well attended and many are beginning the Christian life.

I had planned to make Thursday the great day of the feast; but Rev. Enoch Foy, who was to preach that evening, is sick and sends word he cannot come. In my extremity I turn to you and ask you to fill the gap without fail.

Knowing how willing you always are to help a brother minister in need, I shall look for you without expecting a reply to this note. Please do not disappoint us. I send this message by Mr. John Boley, who returns to your neighborhood today.

Sincerely yours in the Master's work,

Ezra Thompson.

Jasper Very prayerfully considered the invitation and, as his engagements permitted him to accommodate his good friend Thompson, he decided to preach at the camp meeting. He little dreamed that all his future life was to be colored by that simple note. So often men's destinies turn upon apparently trivial events.

As the journey was long Jasper decided it would be pleasant to have a few of his friends accompany him. So he betook himself to Judge LeMonde's house and asked the Judge and his wife to make two of the party, but they had matters which forbade their going. He then spoke to Viola and George and requested them to go.

Early Thursday morning Jasper Very rang the doorbell at "Mount Pisgah." Miss Viola herself answered the bell and led the preacher into the drawing-room. She gave him this information: "George is to drive six of us to the camp meeting in our three-seated carriage. Miss Stella Nebeker will sit with George; on the middle seat my cousin, Miss Alice LeMonde, and Miss Bertha Nebeker, Stella's sister; and they have appointed you and me to occupy the third seat. The carriage will be driven up presently and we have a surprise for you; but do not get too excited."

The preacher could not imagine what the surprise was, but he had to possess his soul in patience. He had not to wait long for he presently heard the sound of wheels. He and Viola stepped out on the piazza.

What did he see? Reader, can you guess? No. He saw Velox. The noble horse was on the near side of the carriage and Prince on the off side.

Very cried out: "Of all things, if there isn't Velox! George, you naughty boy, why didn't you tell me? Where did you find him?"

The preacher ran to the splendid creature, proud, sleek and glossy as ever, and put his arm over his neck, and stroked and patted his face. "George you must tell me all about the way you succeeded in getting your horse back to the plantation."

George said: "Hold your horses, pastor, and when we are speeding in the carriage I will the tale relate."

The six were soon seated in the vehicle. George spoke to the willing horses and they were off, through the plantation grounds, along the county road to the river highway up which they were to travel twenty miles. It was a charming day in June and the road now was in fine condition. A gentle shower the night before had laid the dust and brightened the face of nature. The leaves on the stately forest trees were full grown and in perfection. The river to their right sparkled in the bright sunlight.

Presently George began his tale for the special benefit of the preacher, the rest having heard it in more or less detail:

"A few days ago I went down to Paducah to sell a large part of our abundant hay crop. I went to the big warehouse of Youtsey and Fry on one of the principal streets and was talking to Mr. Sydney Youtsey on the sidewalk, when I saw a splendid carriage drawn by two fine bay horses coming along the street. A Sambo, black as the ace of spades, was driving with a high sense of his importance; and in fact he handled the reins and whip like a professional. In the back seat reclined a portly gentleman, dressed in faultless style, and by his side his wife of ample proportions, also garbed in the height of fashion.

"While the turnout was some distance away I was sure that the near horse was Velox. As luck would have it the man in the carriage had some business with Youtsey and Fry and ordered Sambo to drive up to the curb. Greatly excited I cried out to Sydney Youtsey: 'That bay on the left is my Velox.' I hastened to the side of the carriage, and, lifting my hat, said to the man: 'Excuse me, sir, but that horse standing here next to the sidewalk is my animal, named Velox. He was stolen from my father's barn up country a few weeks ago by two desperate thieves. My name is George LeMonde, son of Judge William LeMonde, of 'Mount Pisgah.'"

"The gentleman addressed expressed great surprise at this announcement, saying:"

'This is a very strange statement. For a long time I wanted a mate for my bay horse Hamlet and instructed my groom to visit the livery stables and other places where horses are kept for sale. He tried for weeks to find a suitable match, but without success. At last, going to one of the largest and most reputable stables in Paducah, he saw this animal you claim, and paying a large price for the same, brought him to my plantation just outside of the city.'

"'Probably,' I said, 'the man who brought Velox to the city gave him into the hands of a party who may have sold him to an honest and upright stable keeper from whom you bought the horse.'"

'But how do I know your story is true, that you own this

Edward T. Curnick

horse?' the planter asked.

"I told him if his servant would drive the carriage into the warehouse and unharness the near horse, that I would convince him that he was my animal."

The planter consented, and soon Velox was standing before us entirely free from his harness. I moved away from him about ten feet. Stretching out my right hand open toward him, I said in a quiet tone of voice: 'Come Velox, come to your master.' Instantly the horse walked up to me and touched my hand with his lips. I put my soft felt hat on my head, and spoke to the horse again: 'Come, Velox, and lift my hat off my head.' He walked up to me the second time and, seizing my hat between his teeth, gently raised it from my head.

"This not only surprised the planter and the rest, but was satisfactory proof to him that the bay was my horse."

Mr. Harcourt, for that was the planter's name, remarked: 'These tricks seem to demonstrate that what you claim is true, but I paid a fancy price for this animal, $500, and I do not feel like losing such a sum.'

"'Neither shall you lose it, sir,' said I. 'This very day I will write you a check for the amount, if you will give my Velox to me.'"

"To this Mr. Harcourt agreed. The pair were driven back to his plantation, and that afternoon Sambo brought him to me. I handed him the check to give to his master. Going to a store near by I bought a saddle and bridle and, putting them on Velox, I mounted him and rode him back to 'Mount Pisgah.' And here he is, sound as ever," and George snapped the whip over the trotting pair so that they increased their speed a bit.

The day was bright and balmy, the steeds were willing, and they made good progress. But the drive was long and it was late dinner time when they arrived on the camp ground. They were welcomed by Ezra Thompson and others and, after resting a short time and partaking of a substantial meal for which their long ride had prepared them, they were ready for the afternoon services. These were of the old camp meeting order, and blessed were the results. An earnest preacher handled the Word of God skillfully, and it became the sword of the Spirit which cut through skepticism, indifference, and sin, and pierced the consciences of many. A blessed altar service closed the meeting.

Jasper Very ate only a light supper. Following his usual custom he went into the woods to pray, to meditate, and to get his sermon into order for the evening. When he came back those who saw him were struck with his look. It was something like that of Moses when he came down from the mount. His face seemed to shine with the light of God. Jasper's natural mein was bold, commanding, and aggressive, so that some thought him domineering and severe; but now his manner was full of humility and peace. He was like a man who had seen a vision of eternal love; his soul was filled with a deep sympathy for sinful men and a great yearning to turn them from the error of their ways. Tonight the fighter was gone, and the pleader took his place.

Before he preached the congregation sang that appealing hymn:

"Show pity, Lord; O Lord, forgive."

Viola LeMonde's confidence as a singer had increased with her recent attempts, and tonight her sweet, pure soprano voice rose clear and strong as she sang with the assembled multitude. Jasper Very heard her voice, and it seemed to him sweeter than the note of an angel, and it moved him one step higher in his grand preparation to speak his Master's word. While the eyes of all were fastened upon him he opened the Bible and read the text: "The Spirit and the bride say, Come. And let him that heareth say, Come. And let him that is athirst come. And whosoever will, let him take the water of life freely."

It is impossible for any report to do justice to that sermon. An abstract of it has come down to us; but it is little more than a skeleton, lacking the flesh and blood and abounding life of the original.

Jasper began by describing the apostle John's imprisonment on the Isle of Patmos. There he was in the Spirit on the Lord's day when he heard a voice saying unto him: "Write." John took the flaming pen of inspiration and wrote those wonderful scenes found in the book of Revelation. But before writing his final "Amen" he gives one last, universal, gracious invitation to all men to come to the water of life and be saved. With marvelous unction and power Jasper spoke of the invitation coming from God's Spirit and from his Church, the bride, to all thirsty souls: "Whosoever will, let him take the water of life freely." At this place the preacher reached the climax of his theme. With the full power of his noble voice he brushed away all artificial distinctions among men, crying out that God is no respecter of persons, but that all men are invited to come to him for salvation. In earnest tones he besought his hearers to know that they are all included in the great invitation; the blacks as well as the whites, the poor farmer on the hills as well as the rich planter in the valley, the outcasts from society, such as moonshiners, horse thieves and gamblers, equally with the moral citizen who yet needed a personal deliverance from sin. All that is required is the will to come.

At last his emotions almost overcame him. Like his Master weeping over Jerusalem, this strong man wept before the people. Throwing into his voice much tenderness, sympathy, love, and persuasion, he called upon them to come forward, kneel in the straw, and seek a merciful Savior's pardon. His appeal was with many most effective; and when the conger- gation arose and started a gospel hymn, scores crowded to the altar seeking forgiveness and peace.

For an hour Jasper, Viola, and the rest who had come from "Mount Pisgah" labored with the penitents at the altar. At half past nine o'clock, long before the service closed, they started for home. They were all lifted to a high plane of spiritual experience, and for some time each was busy with his or her own thoughts and few words were spoken. The moon had risen and was throwing her mild light through the thick trees as best she could. Gradually George LeMonde and the three girls got into a more talkative and merry mood. Now and then a happy laugh floated through the forest, and was heard by the wakeful owl as he sat perched on some high branch, or with rush of wings flew through the air seeking his prey. They spoke of the camp meeting and the commoner events of every day life, occasionally asking the opinion of Jasper and Viola concerning this or that event or notion. But George on the front seat was too much occupied with guiding the horses through the uncertain light and with the chat of the fair girl at his side to pay much attention to those in the rear seats, and the two girls in the middle naturally kept their eyes and ears turned forward. This left Jasper and Viola in a measure to themselves. They spoke occasionally to each other, but their words were fewer than their thoughts.

Jasper's heart in the meeting had been aflame with love to

God and his fellowman, and what better soil than that can there be for a man's love for a pure and beautiful woman to spring and grow? All the wealth of his great nature was even then being given to the woman at his side, and he felt the hour had come to make that love known. And Viola was ready to receive it as a most precious gift and in return to offer a yet richer treasure, a woman's unsullied affection.

In that carriage was about to take place the world's most wondrous mystery—two lives, which for months had been drawn together more and more strongly by a power which no man can understand, at last meeting and blending in a union which God in heaven makes and which eternity cannot sever.

Jasper did not need words to express his love nor Viola to receive it. They were more than half way home when Jasper moved his large, honest, chivalrous right hand over to Viola and took her small, beautiful hand in his. She did not resist the act, but let her little hand lie in his broad palm. That was all. Their betrothal was as silent as the meeting of God and a human soul. Words were not needed. They seemed out of place. They would have appeared almost a profanation. In fact they could not then have been spoken. The light carriage robe covered those two hands, and the laughing girls in the next seat did not suspect that just behind them an engagement without words was taking place. What joys, what sorrows, what tragedies and comedies occur so near us that we can almost touch them with our fingers, and yet we are unconscious of their existence?

So they rode along by the quiet river. Sometimes the stream was hidden by high and mighty trees and willows growing by its bank; at other times they saw the placid waters, and the moonbeams shining upon it making a pathway of silver light.

At last the horses turned into the great gateway, the carriage wheels crunched upon the graveled drive, and soon they were before Viola's home. It was very late, after midnight. George took his team to the barn, for he would not call up Mose at that time of night. Alice LeMonde and her two girl friends at once went upstairs.

Viola opened the drawing-room door, and she and Jasper entered. They stood by the piano, leaning against it. She looked up into his face with a happy smile in her deep blue eyes and a tender flush in her pink cheeks. Jasper, gazing down upon her with inexpressible feelings of reverence and love, imprinted a kiss upon her pure brow, thus sealing their unspoken troth. They walked together to the broad staircase where they parted bidding each other good-night.

CHAPTER XX

KIDNAPPED

The hour was late the next morning when Jasper Very awoke from a refreshing sleep. At first the incidents of the past night did not arrange themselves in proper order before his mind, but soon the succession of events and their meaning became clear. He arose, dressed, attended to his ablutions and devotions, and sat down to think. This was the tenor of his thoughts: "What a fortunate being I am to have gained the love of this true and noble woman. I feel myself unworthy of such affection and confidence. A new idea of God has come to me. He gives himself for those whom he loves. And in a new sense I am willing to sacrifice my all for her whom I love. Heretofore I have looked to my own interests as to food, clothing, lodging, and other things. Perhaps I have been a bit selfish. Now I shall delight also to plan for her well-being and happiness. When the marriage rite is said, how gladly shall I promise to 'love, comfort, and keep her in sickness and in health, to bestow upon her my worldly goods, and to keep her only unto myself.' Jasper, a precious treasure has been entrusted to your keeping, a treasure the most valuable on earth, and you must be careful to keep it from all harm."

At this moment his soliloquy was interrupted by a knock at

the door, and Nora's announcement: "Please, sur, breakfast is waitin' fer yo' in de dinin' room."

"Thank you, Nora, I shall be down presently." And he descended the stairs without loss of time.

You ask, reader, what were the thoughts of Miss Viola when she awoke from her deep sleep? As the writer is a man he cannot tell. No man can sound the depths of a woman's heart. She only can understand her motives, her desires, her modes of thinking, her varying moods. She holds the key to the inner chambers of her nature, and no masculine hand can seize that key and unlock those apartments.

However, we believe we are able to fathom some of the ideas which passed through our heroine's mind that bright morning. We can take it for granted that she was very happy; that the future looked very promising, though she was impressed by the responsibility of becoming a minister's wife.

When Jasper Very descended the stairs and entered the dining-room he found Viola and her mother awaiting him, the rest having eaten some time before. The ladies cordially greeted their guest, and the meal was partaken of with a seasoning of pleasant conversation.

After breakfast the twain went into the drawing-room, and there the stalwart preacher took his own darling into his arms, and for the first time their lips met in a rapturous kiss. They sat side by side on the beautifully upholstered sofa, and looked the splendid couple they were.

If the night before, silence was golden, surely this morning speech was silver. Jasper said: "Viola, my dear, I am giving a new meaning to that Scripture passage: 'This is my

Edward T. Curnick

commandment, that ye love one another.'" "And I," replied Viola, "feel like expressing as my sentiment those words in the Song of Songs: 'My beloved is mine, and I am his.'" "Well," said the parson, "we must seal that ownership with another kiss." It was readily given and received, and we are afraid several more followed to keep the first company.

Then they fell to talking about the future: how they hoped some day to establish a home of their own; how they would walk hand in hand through life bearing its burdens, and meeting the exacting duties of the ministry with mutual helpfulness.

Thus they conversed for a long time on the new and opening vistas of life. At length Viola said: "Jasper dear, let us take a walk this fine morning toward the great knob, and enjoy together the beauties of nature. It seems as though nature itself would delight to shower its blessing upon us."

Jasper was willing, and they went as before to the apple orchard, but instead of stopping there they climbed the ascent to the foot of the knob. Then they entered the woods which covered the great elevation from near its base to the top. They emerged into a zigzag foot-path, difficult to follow, and climbed up and up. Many times the strong arm of Jasper had to help the maiden at his side to surmount steep and bush-entangled places.

At last after much exertion they reached the top of the knob, where they beheld a wide-extended view. Below them lay Judge LeMonde's broad plantation and many others on the right hand and on the left. Beyond these ran the beautiful river through the landscape like a ribbon of silver, and they saw in the far distance valleys and hills and majestic knobs, making altogether a picture of surpassing loveliness.

The man and the woman were enchanted with the scene and Jasper, full of deep emotions, cried out: "Bless the Lord, O my soul: and all that is within me, bless his holy name. He watereth the hills from his chambers; the earth is satisfied with the fruit of thy works. He causeth the grass to grow for the cattle, and herb for the service of man."

Viola exclaimed: "My father's plantation is called 'Mount Pisgah,' and this view reminds me of that other scene Moses saw on his 'Mount Pisgah.'"

They sat under one of the great forest trees crowning the brow of the knob and feasted their eyes on the near and the distant prospect. They heard the birds singing in the trees, and saw the saucy squirrels running up and down the hickory and other trees. Jasper spoke of his present engagements, saying on that afternoon he must visit a family down the river, and the next day he had an appointment to begin a two days' meeting in a distant township of the county.

Viola told of her plans. She intended tomorrow morning to have Mose drive her to a number of the families attending the mission school. She wished to become better acquainted with them, to show a friendly interest in their welfare, and to teach the boys and girls some further rudiments of knowledge, and tell them a number of interesting Bible stories.

This knowledge gave Jasper much concern, and he said: "My dear Viola, I have now even more than a pastor's regard for your safety and welfare. Are you not afraid to travel those lonely hills without any protector save Mose? While the mission school gradually is improving the moral tone of that region, you know there are some depraved and desperate persons living about there who would not hesitate to steal your horses, or your purse, or commit other crimes, if it were

Edward T. Curnick

to their seeming advantage to do so?"

"Yes, I know that, dear Jasper, but hitherto the Lord has protected me, and I believe I can trust him to hold me safely in the hollow of his almighty hand. If I am called to suffer in his cause, I am willing. I have no fear of physical violence, and I am sure duty calls me to that settlement tomorrow."

"Well, my beloved, may heaven still safeguard you, and may you continue to be a blessing to that community which needs reformation, education and the gospel so much."

Viola spoke: "It is getting near dinner time, and we must not be late for that meal as we were for breakfast." With that they arose, and proceeded down the knob and on to the mansion.

After dinner Jasper Very bade them all a cordial good-by, and proceeded on his errand of mercy to a family who needed his ministrations.

Early the next morning Viola, seated in her phaeton with faithful Mose holding the reins over Prince and Bess, started to the mission school settlement. She had taken with her some things which would interest the children—candy for the little ones and some bright books for those older. The distance was considerable, but at last they arrived at the cabin of Mart Spink, where they were cordially received.

Viola stepped down from the carriage and, entering the house, soon had the whole family around her. Their minds seemed famished for knowledge. She first opened a paper bag and passed several pieces of candy to the younger children, Elmira, Robert and Jonathan. She offered the bag to the parents and to Susanna, and they helped themselves sparingly. She then brought out from her satchel a nicely bound copy of Aesop's Fables, and presented the book to Susanna. The girl was both surprised and pleased. Opening her wonderful eyes wide, she thanked her teacher in few words. Viola also gave the family some of the simpler school books used in the public schools and a few volumes of a religious nature. After a further half hour spent in pleasant conversation Viola left the cabin, and directed Mose to drive to the Sneath home.

She found Harrop Sneath sitting under the shade of a tree about as lazy and contented as ever. He was smoking tobacco contained in a corncob pipe. But Viola noticed a decided improvement in the cabin. It was cleaner than when she first saw it, and had a bit more of furniture in it. All the children showed the benefit they had received from attending the mission school. Jemima, the oldest daughter, revealed the greatest improvement. Her eye was brighter, her dress cleaner and better fitting, and her demeanor showed more intelligence and self-possession.

Viola distributed sweets and books to this family much as she had done to the other, and they were gladly received. She led the talk to things which would interest their minds—prospects for good crops, the sewing circle recently organized for women and girls, the picnic which the mission school expected soon to have.

She told them several thrilling Bible stories about David slaying Goliath, Daniel in the lions' den, the three Hebrew children.

It was nearing dinner time and the mother invited Viola to partake of their plain fare. She said: "You air u'st to all de good tings money can buy. We'uns cayn't gibe you much, but sich as we'uns hab you air welcome to."

Viola replied: "I am really greatly obliged to you, Mrs. Sneath, for your kind invitation, and will gladly dine with you today. It is not so much the amount or kind of food one is given but the spirit in which it is given that counts."

"Jist so," said Mrs. Sneath, "so we'uns'll all set down soon to corn pone and pork. Please ask your nigger to unhitch his hosses and put 'em in de bawn. He'll find sum hay der for 'em. De nigger shall hab sum dinner too."

Viola putting aside any punctilious feelings she had, partook of the homely meal with what grace and relish she could command, and thanking them all for their kindness, bade them good-by.

Viola visited a number of other families in the afternoon, and toward the evening of the long summer day instructed her servant to turn the horses toward home. They were not far from the cabin of the monster dwarf, Zibe Turner. A strange feeling of fear and apprehension sprang up within her. Was it caused by her nearness to the home of this wicked man, or by a premonition of danger?

They were passing through one of the densest parts of the great forest. The sun was yet some distance above the horizon, but his slanting rays could throw only a dim light through that mass of wood and foliage.

Suddenly two men sprang from behind high bushes by the roadside. They had black cloth masks over their faces. Holes were cut in the masks through which the bandits could see. One man was tall and broad. The other was short and thickset. The shorter man leaped to the horses' heads and, seizing the reins, stopped their progress. The other stepped to the side of the phaeton, and said in a voice he tried to disguise: "Lady, we'uns do not mean to harm you, but you must cum wid us."

Viola, though dreadfully frightened, straightened herself up in the carriage, and replied: "What do you men mean by stopping a carriage on the highway, and thus disturbing peaceable citizens? I call upon you to go, let go the reins of my horses, and allow my servant to drive me home."

"Dat is fur from our wish," said the desperado, "and if you won't walk away quietly wif us, we'uns will have to tote you away."

With this the highwayman (who was no other than Sam Wiles) jumped into the vehicle, and seizing the young woman around the waist, was dragging her forcibly to the ground. Viola could make no successful resistance in the grasp of this powerful man, but he met resistance where he little expected it. The slave held the buggy whip in his hand, and hastily reversing his hold on the whip, brought the butt end of it down with much force on the miscreant's head. Wiles was half stunned by the blow, but he would not release his hold on Viola, and cursed the black with dreadful oaths.

But it was the work only of a second for the terrible dwarf, Zibe Turner, to spring to the front of the carriage, and grabbing Mose in his sinuous arms, he drew him to the earth, then struck him a terrific blow on his head, and threw him to the ground. What the blow might not have done (for a negro's skull is very thick) the fall accomplished; for when he fell Mose's head struck the protruding root of a great oak tree, and the blow was of sufficient violence to stun the black man. Zibe Turner let the negro lie by the side of the road, and going to the horses led them to a trunk of a tree and, taking the hitch strap, tied it to a lower limb. The outlaws' purpose this time was not stealing horses.

Edward T. Curnick

In the meantime Sam Wiles carried Viola, vainly struggling, about one hundred feet up the road and turned to the right, where not far away a two-seated wagon stood, with two horses hitched to it. Wiles lifted Viola, now exhausted and half dead with fear, into the rear seat and sat down beside her. Presently the monster dwarf appeared and, freeing the horses, jumped on to the front seat. Turning the horses into the road, he drove in an opposite direction to that which Viola had been taking.

No words were spoken by any of the party and the horses pursued their way through the darkening forest. After a time they were driven by the dwarf into the enclosure before his mother's cabin. She was at the door, evidently expecting them. The devil which was in her caused her to cry out in hideous glee: "An' so you'uns cotched her did you'uns? Good. Now we'uns'll see what de Jedge'll do. Will he put gentl'men ob de hills in de jug ag'in? De debil blast 'im and all his kind." Looking at Viola, who now had braced herself for any approaching ordeal, remembering that she was Judge LeMonde's daughter, the hag said: "Now, my purty lady, we'uns'll see who'll wear fine clothes, an' eat de best tings, an' go round de kentry convartin' de people. We'uns count dat you'll get a taste of how we'uns live. Don't hurt yer digestion ner spile yet purty looks longin' ter see yer pa an' ma an' dat cussed preacher."

The monster dwarf here broke in, speaking in his deep voice: "Ma, dat's nuff now. Tell sis to git ready in a hurry, for we'uns have a long drive before us."

Sis was soon ready—the tall, raw-boned, homely young woman, a fit member of this ogre family, but with a little less of depravity in her makeup and looks. She was dressed in a long calico gown, heavy coarse shoes, and a much worn hat, whose flowers appeared worse than "the last rose of summer," after it had faded.

Viola maintained silence, and awaited developments. The plan soon unfolded itself. Sis Turner got up into the rear seat beside Viola. Zibe Turner mounted to the front seat, took the reins in his right hand, spoke to the horses, and away they went, leaving Sam Wiles looking after them. What was the character of his thoughts?

Turner drove his team along a faintly marked country road always toward higher ground. On and on they went for miles, the way in many places becoming so dark, that the only direction was the avenue made by the cutting down of the trees. Sometimes they came to such serious obstructions in the road that the driver had to get down to remove them. At last the way was so narrow they had to leave the wagon and proceed on horseback.

After climbing higher and higher they arrived at a small open place near the top of the knob. In its midst was a diminutive log cabin, consisting of only one room. Turner stopped his horses in front of the cabin, dismounted, and requested the girls to do the same. He unbarred the door, and the three entered. By means of flint, steel, tinder, and burnt rags Turner made a light. Viola observed that the cabin was of about the same order as the Sneath home she had visited that morning. A large fireplace was on one side. There was no window, and only one door. Two cheap beds were in two corners of the room. In another corner there were a number of bundles of provisions. A few cooking utensils were on the hearth, and a few dishes were on the table. The door on the inside was secured by a heavy bar which fell into a strong socket, the bar being fastened by a stout padlock.

Zibe Turner spoke: "Miss LeMonde, dis cabin is to be yer hum for a while. My sister is to be comp'ny for ye, an' also

Edward T. Curnick

yer guard. No harm is to cum to ye, if ye do what ye air told. I'm goin' to leave now, an' sis'll tend to yer wants. Good-night to bof uv you'uns."

With this he left the cabin, and drove away.

CHAPTER XXI

THE SEARCH

As the time for the evening meal was approaching at Judge LeMonde's mansion, his wife said to him: "I wonder what is keeping Viola so long today. She told me before starting, she would be home by sundown, and it surely is time she were back."

The Judge responded: "Do not be alarmed. She may have been kept longer than she expected at some of the places she visited. The days are very long now, and the twilight lingers. Besides, there will be moonlight tonight and if they are delayed they can easily see their way over the big road by the light of the moon. Mose is a trustworthy fellow and we know he is a careful driver."

At this time Nora knocked at the door, announcing that supper was ready. Madam LeMonde was not fully at ease, but went with the rest to the dining-room. The repast was rather a quiet one, and when it was finished dusk had fully settled over the valley. The Judge and his wife went to the piazza and looked down the plantation private way, but could see no sign of carriage or horses. They together walked to the large gate which opened on the county road, opening the gate, and went the short distance to the river road along

Edward T. Curnick

which the returning carriage would come. They stood and strained their eyes looking down the highway, but could discern no vehicle of any kind approaching.

For some time they stood looking and listening, and then returned to the house. Now they were anxious indeed; and so was their son George who had been to the barn on some business with one of the hostlers.

Madam LeMonde exclaimed: "What can be keeping them? Surely some accident or harm has befallen them. Viola would never stay away from home as late as this unless she had company with her. I am very nervous and disturbed. What can we do?"

George spoke up and said: "Do not be distressed, mother. If the carriage does not come in a few minutes, I will get Velox and ride along the road to meet it and to be of help, if it is needed."

"Do so, my son, for this will help to relieve me of suspense," said his mother.

They waited until it was quite dark, for the moon had not yet risen, though it would show itself presently. Then George decided to go at once. Hurrying to the barn, he saddled and bridled his noble horse and instantly went along the road, his horse trotting rapidly.

About five miles down the road George met Mose coming in the phaeton, but Viola was missing. Terribly anxious for the safety of his sister, the white man asked the slave what had happened.

Mose was still somewhat dizzy from the blow he had received from the monster dwarf and his fall on the root of the oak, but he told the story as far as he knew, and added some particulars about himself.

He said he lay for a long time unconscious by the side of the country road, but at last his senses came back to him. His head pained him very much, and a great swelling was over his right eye. In the dim light he saw the horses hitched under the tree.

He tried to rise from the ground, but found it impossible at first. After making a number of attempts, he managed to get up on his feet and went to the phaeton reeling like a drunken man. He untied the horses and almost fell into the seat. He managed, however, to keep the horses in the road and drove them as best he could till he met "Mas'r George."

George considered whether it were better for him to ride furiously after the outlaws, or to return to the plantation with Mose. He chose the latter course, and before a great while they came up the private way to the mansion.

The Judge and his wife, and indeed the whole household, were anxiously awaiting them. When the phaeton drove up and no Viola in it, Madam LeMonde became hysterical and almost fainted. She screamed: "Where is my daughter? Where is she? What has happened to her? Tell me quickly."

The Judge was compelled to quiet his wife before he could hear the story of his daughter's abduction.

The group returned into the house. Entering the sitting-room they discussed what was best to be done. The Judge requested his son George to ride as fast as possible to the county seat, arouse the sheriff and ask him to select a posse as soon as he was able, to search for the missing girl. This George proceeded to do. He rushed to the barn and mounting a fresh horse set off at all speed on his errand.

Judge LeMonde hastily wrote some notes containing a brief account of his daughter's seizure and, entrusting them to his most faithful slaves, instructed them to deliver the notes to those addressed. These were his most intimate neighbors and friends in the valley. He requested them to meet him at "Mount Pisgah" early in the morning.

As the Judge could do no more that night he suggested that they retire to their rooms, and seek rest. This they did, but no sleep came to him nor to his wife that night. Their thoughts were with the girl:

"Where is she? Have they murdered her? What could be their object in carrying her away? Was it revenge? How difficult it will be to find her. But Oh! that morning would come, so that the attempt can be made!"

Thus they beat the walls of darkness with unavailing questions, and even their prayers were mixed with natural forebodings and fears.

With the first dawn of day Nora, who also had passed a restless night, awoke the fat cook (for she in spite of sympathy for the family had slept soundly) and asked her to get coffee and toast as quickly as possible. This was soon prepared, and the Judge and his wife drank the stimulant and ate a little toast.

Presently thereafter the neighbors began to arrive. They were greatly affected by the foul deed, and vowed the direst punishment upon the outlaws in case they were captured. They offered to the family every assistance in their power. They spoke comforting words to the afflicted Judge, who showed the marks of his mental anguish and sleepless night in his haggard face. They sent their respects to Madam LeMonde, who was too prostrated to see them at this time.

When all were arrived it was decided to await the coming of the sheriff and posse when all would go to the spot where Viola was taken, and from that point scour the wilderness under the sheriff's lead.

The sun was not high in the heavens when the sheriff and a company of eight determined-looking men rode up to the mansion. No words were wasted. All were eager to depart. The leader ordered the company and planters to fall in, and away they went with swift pace toward the place they sought. Judge LeMonde and George rode with the sheriff. Mose, nearly recovered from his hurt, was in the company as guide.

They came to the place where the carriage was stopped, and Mose took time to point to the very spot where his head came in contact with the root of the oak. They followed the road along which Sam Wiles went with the struggling Viola in his arms. They turned to the right, and saw the hoof prints of the horses the marauders had hidden with the wagon in the brush.

Examining the road carefully (a road very little traveled) they saw wagon tracks which might have been those made by the wagon in which the kidnappers sat with their victim.

Suspecting that the men would go first to the cabin of Zibe Turner, they went to this house, and found the old mother at home. From her they could get no satisfaction. She denied that she had seen Viola LeMonde lately. Shaking her bony arm at the Judge and the rest, she commanded them to begone from her premises.

The searchers, leaving the enclosure, rode a short distance into the woods and there stopped. They decided to follow the flight as before by means of the horse hoof and wagon tracks. This they did, but soon the way became merely a path, and then the path ended in the unmarked woodland.

All trace of the fugitives was thus lost. The sheriff then divided his company into parties of two men each, and sent them in different directions in such a manner as to cover as much ground as possible. Before dismissing them, he told them to search diligently the ground traversed, especially the wildest and deepest parts of the hills. They were to ride their horses when the way permitted, otherwise to go on foot.

Not one of these men needed urging. They were all fired with a grim determination to find if possible the place where the beautiful captive was imprisoned. They took no account of their own personal affairs, of hunger and fatigue, of the difficulties of travel through the uncleared forests. The clothing of some became torn with briers and sharp rocks, their shoes were damaged with stones, fallen limbs, muck and mire. Their hands were pierced by many thorns, as they pushed their way through the wilderness.

The first day passed without finding any trace of the missing maiden.

Where was Jasper Very while these thrilling events were taking place? As we have intimated, he had gone to a distant part of the county to hold a two days' meeting. All unconscious of the terrible evil that had fallen upon his betrothed, he was pursuing his Master's work with his accustomed zeal and success.

Before leaving home to visit her mission school people Viola had informed her mother of the new and intimate relations existing between Jasper Very and herself. The mother was much pleased with the engagement and, woman like, could not keep the news from her husband. She told him the story. He also was pleased with the information. The night he sent word to his neighbors of the abduction he wrote a longer note to Jasper Very, acquainting him of the villainous occurrence. This message he sent to the preacher by a trustful servant, Joshua.

The servant rode through the night, but did not reach the village till the middle of the next morning. Horse and man were very much exhausted. The eight o'clock meeting was just closing and the preaching service was about to begin, when Joshua rode up to the little meeting-house. Jasper, looking through the open door, saw Joshua, whom he knew as one of Judge LeMonde's slaves.

Thinking something was wrong, Jasper hurried from the church and spoke to the messenger. Joshua gave him the note. As he read its contents, a heavy groan escaped his lips and he almost fell to the ground. With a tremendous effort at self-control, but with tears coursing down his manly cheeks, he said to Joshua: "Man, you and your horse are very tired. A livery stable is just around the corner. Put up your horse there, and the owner will tell you where you can get food and rest."

He then went into the church and said: "Friends, I have just received news which is very urgent, requiring my presence in another part of the county. I am sorry I cannot preach here this morning, but I must be excused, and I will ask the Rev. Irby Trynor kindly to take my place." With these words he hurried from the building, and going to the stable of his stopping-place, quickly put saddle and bridle on trusty Bob, and rode like a Jehu in the direction of "Mount Pisgah."

Edward T. Curnick

Darkness was settling on the river bottom when Jasper Very came along the road passing by Judge LeMonde's plantation. Riding to the corner he turned to the right, went up the county road to the big gate, opened it, and passed up to the piazza. The Judge and George had returned from their unsuccessful search a half hour before. The planters had gone home for the night, promising to renew the hunt next morning. The sheriff and his men were accommodated at various houses, some stopping at "Mount Pisgah."

As Jasper dismounted the Judge himself met him. For a moment the two strong men could find no words to speak. They shook hands together and looked the sorrow they felt. Then the Judge invited Jasper into the house, ordering a servant to take Bob to the barn. Jasper was most anxious to know all the particulars of the case, and the Judge told him every detail. Their tired, hungry bodies craved some refreshments which were served to them, and soon they went to their rooms to seek that rest which the strenuous efforts of the morrow required.

In the quiet of his room Jasper had a great fight with his own heart. Fierce temptations assailed him. He would have vengeance. If he found those atrocious men he would kill them, if he could. His feelings found vent in some of the imprecatory psalms. Such cattle as Wiles and Turner were not fit to live; they polluted the earth upon which they stood. If arrested, they should suffer the direst penalties of the law.

But after this paroxysm had spent itself, his feeling became calmer. Prayer, like a healing balm, came to his aid. He was able to commit even this trial to the wisdom and help of almighty God.

Thus he found repose in sleep, and in the morning arose with a clear mind, a refreshed body, and a preparation for the heavy duties of the day.

That day the search was renewed with the same vigor as yesterday, but even with the help of Very, who passed through the wilderness like a tornado, the hiding place of the desperadoes was not discovered.

The searchers returned to their abodes well nigh exhausted and discouraged. Judge LeMonde requested Jasper Very to pass the night at "Mount Pisgah," and this the preacher did.

After supper they were sitting on the piazza going over the incidents of the day, and planning what course they would best take on the morrow, when one of them, looking in the direction of the big gate, saw a light shining apparently on one of its posts. He called the attention of the rest to it. They wondered what it could mean. It could not be a firefly. It was not the light of a lantern in the hands of some one walking; the light was too steady. The Judge said to George: "My son, run down the lane, and see what that light means." George needed no urging, but at once went with swift pace to the gate. There he beheld a lighted candle stuck on the top of the right post of the gate. Below the candle was a piece of paper tied with a string, and the string made fast to the post.

George brought both candle and paper to the group on the piazza. The Judge took the paper into the sitting room. On the paper was some writing done with a sprawling hand. He had some difficulty in deciphering it, but at last made out its contents. This is how it read:

> "judg lemond yer Dater iz wel and in Gud hans. You must gib 1000 dollars in Gold and She wil kum hum put Mony in Holler Tre whar Riber Bens 4 mile belo bridge-water nex Mundy Eve. If de Man Who Kums for de Gold gits shot or tuk yer Dater wil dy.

"Sind Po Wite."

Judge LeMonde was some time deciphering the note. When he understood it, he called the sheriff and the other men into the room, and read aloud the writing. At once a council was held. The Judge said: "Evidently the bandits have put the time of payment next Monday evening to give me opportunity to get the money from the bank. Sheriff, what do you advise?"

The officer thought deeply for a while, and then answered: "Those are very desperate and determined men. Their reason for abducting your daughter is now plain—it was for ransom. Of course, Judge, you do not put one thousand dollars in the scale against Miss Viola's life. It is outrageous to think of gratifying the wishes of those scoundrels, but I am afraid it must be done, if we cannot circumvent them before that time. We have still tomorrow and Monday to continue the search. Perhaps we can discover their hiding place in these two days."

Jasper Very said: "We must be more diligent, if possible, than before in seeking the captive. Tomorrow is the Sabbath, but I feel it my duty to give up all my church engagements to help find the missing one."

"Tomorrow," added the sheriff, "we will cover new territory in the forest, and let us hope for success."

CHAPTER XXII

THE RESCUE

While the men at "Mount Pisgah" were planning how to deliver Viola from her captors, Mart Spink, father of Susanna, the girl with the wonderful eyes, was down with a severe chill in his cabin among the hills. Cold shivers ran up and down his back, as though a lizard shod with ice were making a playground of it. Then the cold struck his head, and his teeth began to chatter worse than if he were climbing "Greenland's icy mountains." Soon his whole body was in a frigid state which made him cry out for bedclothes, and more bedclothes, and still more blankets and quilts. He shook so with his chilly sensations that the bedclothes above him were in perpetual motion, and the mattress under him was agitated with the motions of his body. Then came on the terrible fever, which was worse than the chill, as the pain of fire is harder to bear than the cold of ice. Poor Spink seemed to be burning up. A dreadful headache seized him, which was only a little relieved when his wife applied cloths wrung out of cold water to his forehead. After some hours came the great sweat, which saturated his night shirt and a portion of his pillow and bedclothes.

This attack was so violent it bordered on a "congestive chill," which the settlers knew to be very dangerous. His wife

Edward T. Curnick

waited upon him all night, not wishing to keep the children up, and in the morning he was very weak and she much worn.

Susanna rose early and took the pail to milk Brindle. What was her surprise to find the barn door open, and when she looked into the building she saw that their young horse, Chester, was missing. He had pushed the barn door ajar and disappeared. She dropped her pail, ran into the house, and told her mother the news. Mrs. Spink thought it best to inform her husband of the occurrence, though he was still quite ill.

Spink spoke from his bed: "That hoss has prob'ly went back to his old hum. You'uns knows I bought him of a feller away back on de knobs. Sum one must go find 'im. I can't go, nuther can yer ma. Elmiry an' the boys must do the chores. So, Susanna, you must get Maud out'n de barn, an' go after de hoss. It's a long trip, an' I'm sorry ye hav ter go. Take a snack (food) with yer, fer ye'll git hungry."

Susanna replied: "Don't be troubled, pa. I can ride as good as a man. I will gladly go, and try my best to find Chester." Her marvelous eyes shone with a brilliant light, and in a few minutes she was gone.

The girl's quest for the horse might have reminded her of Saul's search for his father's asses, had she been better acquainted with the Bible. As Saul failed to discover the animals, but found a kingdom, so the maid did not find the horse, Chester, but discovered a startling situation.

Her way led by Zibe Turner's cabin, then to the knob, and along its side, ever up toward the former home of the horse. When she had nearly reached the top she came to the little open space containing the hut in which Viola LeMonde was imprisoned.

There was an old well by the hut, but its sweep had rotted down, and the water was stagnant and unfit to drink. Hence, Elmira Turner, the guard of Viola, was compelled to go to a spring one-eighth of a mile distant to get pure water. Having barred the cabin on the outside, she was on such a trip when Susanna rode up.

The rider, with a girl's curiosity, came to the hut to look it over. Viola heard the horse's tread and, looking between two logs from which the chinks had fallen, saw her young friend. "Susanna, dear," she cried, greatly excited, "Sam Wiles and Zibe Turner have taken me by force and brought me here. My guard, Elmira Turner, has gone to the spring for water. Ride as fast as you can, and tell my father or some other friend of my whereabouts."

Susanna was surprised beyond measure at the discovery, and her heavenly eyes glowed like two stars.

"O my dear teacher," she exclaimed, "I have heard that you were carried away. I wanted to help in the search but was not able. This is awful. I will ride back as quick as possible, and try to find some one to come to aid you."

With this she turned her horse about, and applied whip and spur to Maud. Regardless of obstructions frequently in her path—fallen limbs, saplings growing close together, bushes coming to the breast of her steed, springy soil and uneven ground—she rode with a swift pace. Her dark hair streamed behind her. With firm hands she held the reins, and her bright eyes traced the direction to take and also looked for some of the searchers.

She was riding through a thick wood, tolerably free from

Edward T. Curnick

underbrush, when she was overjoyed to see Jasper Very riding toward her on his well known horse, Bob. The preacher showed the marks of his exertions. His face was flushed, his hair never very amenable to brush and comb, was rumpled by contact with bushes, twigs and leaves. He was moving along swiftly, ever looking for some signs which would lead him to his beloved. He had become separated from his companion, John Larkin.

Susanna and Jasper saw each other about the same time, and in a trice their horses were face to face. Almost breathless with hard riding and excitement the girl told what she had learned.

The preacher was affected as though a current of electricity had passed through his body. For a minute he was too bewildered to think, but by an effort of will he became somewhat more calm and considered what was best to be done.

He said: "Susanna, how can we thank you enough for this information? God bless you for bringing it to me. Now ride as rapidly as possible to your home and ask your father please to loan us a horse and buggy. Bring them along the road as far as you can with ease. If I get Miss Viola out of the hut, I will give her a place on Bob's back, and we will ride till we meet the buggy. Is it possible for you to direct me to the hut?"

"Yes, Mr. Very. When I returned, thinking I might have to act as pilot to the cabin I kept the way in my mind, and I think I can tell you pretty well how to go." She then indicated the route in considerable detail, and Jasper was sure he could find the place.

What deep emotions stirred his breast as he hurried forward!

He knew that his darling was alive. This was a great satisfaction. But she was in dire peril. He must rescue her at once at all hazards. He would dare the danger alone, for the searchers being scattered through the wilderness, there was no one to whom he could look for help.

He had learned that Elmira Turner, the monster dwarf's sister, was guarding Viola, and he rightly supposed that Sam Wiles or the dwarf would picket the hut most of the time.

Without any great difficulty Jasper Very followed the route given him by Susanna. At last he saw a little before him the opening in the forest of which he had been told. He dismounted from Bob, and hid him in a thicket. Then he cautiously crept forward and, coming to the edge of the clearing, screened himself behind a big walnut tree and reconnoitered the surroundings. The coast seemed clear. He walked quickly to the door of the hut and said in a loud voice: "Viola, Jasper is here, and has come to take you home. I find the door is locked on the inside, but not the outside. Can you unfasten the door?"

"O Jasper," said Viola, "the woman with me holds the key to the lock, and she will not give it to me."

"No, indeed, I'll not," said Elmira Turner, "an' I defy you to git in. My brother'll be here soon, an' if you want to save yer hide, it will be healthy for you to make yo'self sca'se right off."

"Woman," shouted Very, "if you will not unlock the door I'll break it down."

"Try it," said she.

Jasper did try. He was the strongest man in the county, and it seemed that now the strength of ten men was given him.

The door was made of thick oak. The cabin may have been built extra strong to shelter some former inmates, if attacked by Indians. But at this time the door was weakened by age and exposure to the elements; also it was somewhat worm eaten.

Jasper put his right shoulder to the door, and pushed with all his might. The door cracked a little, but did not break. He took the broken well sweep and, using the larger end (which contained some sound wood) as a battering ram, fiercely assaulted the obstruction. This weakened the structure, but it did not yield. Then Jasper, summoning all his mighty strength, hurled himself against the door, and it fell in with a crash.

He at once passed inside the hut. Taking hold of Viola, he was leading her to the opening, when Elmira Turner, seized hold of the girl to keep her in the room. A struggle ensued. Jasper did not want to strike the Turner woman or treat her roughly. So he was compelled to force Viola from her grasp by main strength. This he did, and taking his betrothed in his arms, stepped out into the sunlight.

Just then the sound of a shot rang out on the stillness of the summer air, and Viola became limp and apparently lifeless in her lover's arms.

Zibe Turner, the monster dwarf, had come to the clearing in the nick of time. He saw the open door. He beheld the rescuer bearing out the captive in his arms. Murder sprang up at once in his heart. He decided to kill the preacher then and there. This he had wanted to do for a long time. But the excitement of the occasion and his own dreadful hate unsteadied his nerves a trifle. When putting his rifle to his shoulder, he aimed at Very's heart, crying out: "Dat's my holt!" The bullet missed its mark, and entered the right shoulder of the lovely Viola.

When the dwarf saw the unexpected result of his shot, even his resolution failed him, and he proceeded no further with his murderous work.

Jasper Very looked down on the senseless form of his beloved, and cried out in the bitter agony of his soul: "My God, my God, why hast thou forsaken me?"

Holding her as he would a little child in his arms, he strode out of the clearing. Quickly coming to his horse, Bob, he unhitched his rein, and holding the unconscious girl tenderly but firmly in his left arm, he swung into the saddle.

With anguish in his soul and unaccustomed tears in his blue eyes, he pressed one kiss upon the pale lips of her who was dearer to him than life. Holding her in as comfortable position as possible, he started down the knob.

Viola gave little if any signs of life. She was wholly unconscious, her face was as pale as death, her eyes were closed, there was no perceptible pulse.

Jasper rode as carefully as possible, but was a considerable time reaching the more open section of the country. At last he came to the very primitive road along which he had not ridden far, when he beheld approaching the horse and buggy he had requested Susanna to get.

Susanna was the driver, and was amazed at what she saw— her Sunday School teacher lying like one dead on the preacher's arm.

Time was too precious for many words of explanation, and it was the work of only a minute or two to place Viola in the buggy, and for Jasper to get in beside her. Susanna rode Bob.

Jasper Very's plan was to take the wounded maiden to Mart Spink's house, and then to hurry for medical help, if she were living.

Driving as rapidly as was consistent with the seriousness of the case, they at last reached the home of Susanna. The daughter rushed into the house and told her mother the tragic story in brief. The woman was greatly shocked, and at once went to the buggy and told Jasper Very that Viola could be put into a bedroom adjoining the one in which her husband lay. Mart Spink was much better now. Such is the way of chills and fever.

Jasper, seeing faint signs of life in Viola, left her to the tender ministries of Mrs. Spink and Susanna, while he rode with all haste for a doctor who lived several miles away.

The women undressed the patient, and put her into the bed. They bathed her wound, and bandaged it as best they could. Fortunately it had not bled excessively.

In due time the physician, who was also a surgeon, came. He probed for the ball, and succeeded in extracting it. He gave those restoratives and remedies which the state of medicine in those days and in that region warranted. He ordered that the patient be kept perfectly quiet, and that no persons but her mother (who became her nurse) and Mrs. Spink should enter the room.

For days and weeks the life of the lovely girl hung in an even balance. Great was the interest which this calamity aroused in the whole country around. The news of the shooting spread with great rapidity. By night all the searchers had heard of it, and as the kidnaped maiden was found and restored to friends, their work in that particular was done, and most of them returned to their homes.

As the golden autumn days came Viola gained a little strength and was able to be moved to "Mount Pisgah." Here Jasper and her intimate friends were permitted to see her for short periods. Her face was as white as the pillow upon which she lay. Her blue eyes had lost their bright, but not their kind and loving, look. Her golden hair was still beautiful, and it seemed an aureole around her head.

One bright day she felt able to hold a longer conversation than before with her betrothed. Very sat by the bedside, holding the thin white hand. The slender finger could scarce retain the beautiful engagement ring her lover had given her.

"Jasper, dear," she said, "how happy I am that I received the cruel ball instead of you. All the suffering I have gladly borne for your sake. Yes, and if it were my lot to be an invalid while life lasts, I would willingly bear the burden, knowing that by the cross I suffer my beloved is able in the full strength of his manhood to preach the gospel and minister to the wants of human souls. So there are compensations in all the ills of life."

"My precious one," said the preacher, "your words are those of her who lives very near the heart of God. The finest thing in the world is sacrifice and suffering for the benefit of others. But you must put far away the idea of being a constant invalid. Gradually you are regaining your health, and before long we shall see you as lively and jolly as ever. By Christmas time I want to behold roses in your cheeks, and see you skip about like a roe upon the mountains. Keep up a brave, trustful spirit, and I believe all will be well."

He kissed his betrothed tenderly, stroked her beautiful hair, and retired from the room.

CHAPTER XXIII

A BATTLE WITH MOONSHINERS

Sam Wiles and Zibe Turner, the monster dwarf, were not captured by the sheriff and his men. For a number of days after the wounding of Viola LeMonde the officers and others kept a sharp watch on the cabins of both outlaws, and tried to find them in some of the fastnesses of the hills. But the bandits were too cunning for them. They seldom dared to enter their homes, but spent most of their time in the open or in the shelter of the cave where the illicit whisky was made. Some of their confederates were usually near them, ready to give them warning of any officer's approach.

At last the climax came. It was a hot evening in mid-August. Judge LeMonde was sitting under the pine trees, attempting to catch any breeze which might blow from the river when, looking down the road leading to the big gate, he saw a woman approaching.

It was Jemima Sneath, and she was evidently laboring under great excitement. Her eyes were deep sunken and glowed like coals of fire. They showed what was in her heart—jealousy, hate, anger, recklessness, courage, determination. Her thick black hair was loosely put together, stray locks falling here and there about her face and neck.

Edward T. Curnick

"Jedge LeMonde," she said, "I am Jemima Sneath, and I live back in de hills. I hev somethin' I wish to tell you. Can I see you by yerself?"

"Certainly, my good woman," replied the Judge, "let me lead you into my private office."

When they were seated Jemima began her story: "Jedge, I have cum to you for revenge. For more'n two years I have bin Sam Wiles' gal, and a year ago he promised to marry me. I have bin true to 'im and bin willin' to set de day any time. But lately his love for me has growd cold, and he has bin goin' with annoder gal in de hills. Yisterday dis gal and I met and had sum words, and she up and tol' me that Sam Wiles had left me for her. With dis I sprung upon her like a wild cat and tore her clothes, scratched her face, and pulled part of her hair out by de roots. Den I left her and marched straight to Sam's cabin, and asked im if wat de gal said was true. He said it war, dat he had lost his luv for me and put it on Kate Sawyer. Sumthing like a knife seemed to cut my heart, and I wanted to die. I left Sam Wiles, sayin': 'Sam, good-by forever; you have broke my heart, and I'll break yourn.'"

Here the woman's emotions overcame her, and she would have fallen from her chair had not Judge LeMonde caught her. He hastened to a table and, filling a glass with water, brought it to her. This revived her, and again she sat up straight with the blazing fire in her eyes.

The Judge tried to comfort her, saying: "Be composed, woman, and finish your story, and I will help you all I am able."

Jemima replied: "I did not cum here to git help, but revenge. Sam Wiles, Zibe Turner, and der crowd have bin busy for a long time makin' 'licit whisky. I know whar dey make and store it, and I'm willin' to tell you'uns how to git to de place."

"To discover where their still is will greatly please the revenue officers," said Judge LeMonde, "but won't you get yourself into trouble if you tell on your friends?"

"Dey ain't my friens'," she fiercely replied. "I cast off de hull lot; and as to trouble nuthin' can't be so hard to bear as de load I carries now. I wish in my soul I war dead."

Again her feelings almost overcame her; but the Judge spoke kindly to her, and in a few minutes she recovered her composure once more. He then requested her to continue her story.

"Dey make der whisky in Wind Cave," she said and proceeded to describe its location as recorded in a former chapter. "To capture de 'shiners and de whisky de officers must 'sprise both openin's to onct," she continued.

The Judge asked: "Would you be willing to tell me how to find the two ways into the cave?"

"I would tell anything to git even with Sam Wiles," was the reply.

"I am sure the capture of these lawbreakers will be a blessing to all this part of Kentucky," remarked Judge LeMonde, "but I am sorry for the reason you have to tell where they may be found."

At this point he got writing material and, asking the woman clearly to describe the way to the cave's mouths, he wrote as she dictated. We will write the account in her own words: "De big openin' is 'bout twenty feet below de top of Bald Knob. You'uns 'member you'uns kin see from de knob's foot

Edward T. Curnick

his bald head, whar is great rocks and not ary trees. Well, de cave's mouf is in er straight line below dat twenty feet. To fin' de odder openin' you'uns walk from de rocky head of de knob 'long his backbone east for 'bout one hundred feet, and you'uns cum to a tall poplar tree. Go down de hill to de souf fifteen feet, and you'uns'll find a thicket full of brambles, bushes, and leaves. De hole is dar, covered with underbrush and leaves."

Having thanked her for the important information given, Judge LeMonde courteously led her to the door and bade her good evening.

Early next morning he took steps to profit by what he had heard. He sent his son George to tell Jasper Very the news while he himself rode to the county seat to notify the sheriff and revenue officers of the outlaw's rendezvous. That very day a keen, trusted employee of the government was deputed to go over the ground and learn whether the woman's story were true or false. In a day or two he reported that he had discovered the two openings to the cave. It was known that the attempt to capture the moonshiners would be dangerous. They were fearless, desperate men, well armed. It would require skill and courage to take them.

The sheriff and chief revenue officers, knowing that the moonshiners were so formidable in arms, numbers, and location, were anxious to have as large an attacking party as possible. Hence they were glad when Long Tom, Jasper Very, honest David Hester and his sons, Hans Schmidt, the German, John Larkin, George LeMonde, and others were sworn in as constables.

Long Tom's case was peculiar. We will let him put it in his own drawling tones: "Friens, it am like dis. Though I has bin a Christian for months, I could not bring myself to gib away de hidin' places of my ol' pals. It looked too much like treachery and betrayal. P'raps I'm wrong but, if so, you'uns will pardon me. But now de case am diffrunt. Thar hidin' place am knowd, an' it is for de good of de neighborhood an' der own good dat dese men should be caught an' der bizness brok up, an' I'm willin' to be one to bring dis about. So I jine yer company, not to kill dose men, but to try to save der souls."

It was decided to divide the attacking company into two parts, one to approach the large opening of the cave and the other the smaller one. Larkin, Grimes and the Hester men were with the former crowd, and Long Tom, Jasper Very, George LeMonde, and Hans Schmidt with the latter. All felt that the best way to begin the attack was to take the moonshiners by surprise, and it was thought that early morning was the most favorable hour, when the outlaws would probably be asleep.

Soon after midnight of a Wednesday morning the men gathered noiselessly at the knob's base, having left their horses far up the road. Just as the first streaks of day were appearing the two groups of men about one hundred feet apart began climbing the steep elevation. The slope was fully forty-five degrees, and in some parts much steeper. The men had to brace their feet against trees and saplings, and near the top to pull themselves up by holding on to branches of trees and shrubs above them.

At last the larger party reached the level, which, extending inward, formed the floor of the cave. The revenue officer peered over the top and saw a man with a rifle by his side asleep with his back braced against a wall. He was near the cave's mouth. Farther he could dimly behold the forms of men lying along the sides of the cave. A smoldering fire was beneath the still, which stood some fifteen feet from

Edward T. Curnick

the entrance.

The officer gave the signal to advance, and sprang upon the ledge with several others. At the same instant the sleeping sentinel awoke, taking in the situation at a glance, seized his rifle and attempted to fire it; but before he could do so the revenue officer was upon him like a tiger upon his prey. Though he could prevent the firing, he could not control the voice, and the man gave one mighty shout, which awoke every sleeper as though the crack of doom had come. They all sprang up in amazement and confusion, and just at this moment the leader called out, "Surrender!" The attacking party, close to their commander's heels, rushed into the cave, and before the outlaws could offer resistance sprang upon them and overpowered most of them.

But Wiles, Turner, and a few others were not to be caught so easily. They were sleeping farther in the cave, and, though awakened so suddenly, did not lose their wits and nerve. They jumped to their feet, and the answer they gave to the summons to surrender was a blaze of rifles, with an instant retreat into the darkness of the cave. The noise of the rifles' discharge reverberated in the cavern like repeated rolls of thunder.

The leader's hat was pierced by a ball, one of his deputies fell shot through the lungs, and honest Hester's second son, Edward, shot through the brain, sank at his father's feet a corpse.

Before the echoes of these shots died away another volley rang out, fired into the darkness at the retreating outlaws. It wounded two or three of them, but most escaped, having turned a corner of the cave before the bullets struck.

Those unhurt, led by Wiles and Turner, made their way as

fast as possible through the darkness to the second opening, for they had no idea that this too had been made known to their pursuers. It was their intention to rush into the forest and then, scattering in several directions, to elude pursuit, and thus escape. Their very precipitency saved some of them in this way. The second company was in its place near the second opening when the men heard the shots of the first attack. Rightly surmising that the moonshiners would try to escape through the second aperture, the men on guard were ready to fire; but they were not prepared to see the renegades rush through the underbrush so swiftly, and, not wishing to shoot them down in cold blood, the leader called: "Halt! Halt! Surrender!"

The outlaws were startled by the cry; but, being desperate, most of them gave no heed to the words. Bending low, they ran with great rapidity to the shelter of the great tree trunks which rose everywhere around. However, some were too late, and the volley which was fired slew several and wounded others.

Wiles, Turner, and three others succeeded in getting behind trees without being injured. The monster dwarf was terrible to behold. He had the quickness of a cat and the fury of a lion. Though the odds were so much against him and the rest, he yelled defiance at the revenue men and volunteers, and cursed them with bitter oaths. They resorted to Indian tactics. They shot from behind trees at any man in sight, and soon had wounded a number. However, the struggle was unequal, for the revenue officer sent his men out in the form of a fan, and thus they would soon have succeeded in making an enfilading fire upon the moonshiners; and the latter could not retreat rapidly, because in running from tree to tree they were in danger of being shot. Besides, in a short time their ammunition was exhausted, and they were at the mercy of their pursuers. When called upon to surrender, all but Wiles

Edward T. Curnick

and Turner complied. These refused.

Then spoke Long Tom with his well known drawl: "Pardners, it would be nuthin' but murder to kill defenseless men, an' I move dat we'uns surround 'em an' bind 'em an' tote 'em off to jail."

This advice was heeded, and Long Tom was the first to move forward. The monster dwarf stood like a wild beast at bay with his clubbed rifle in his hand. As Long Tom came near he swung it with terrible force, attempting to break his adversary's skull; but Tom was too quick and the blow passed by. Instantly Long Tom caught the dwarf around the arms to hold those members, for he well knew their power. But in a moment Turner, like a snake, twisted his right arm loose, and reaching under his short coat, drew out a sharp hunting knife, and hissing the words, "Traitor! Dat's my holt," between his clenched teeth, drove it into the back of the reformed moonshiner.

One man, however, had been on the alert for some dastardly act of the dwarf. This was young George LeMonde. Ever since his horse had been stolen, and his sister had been kidnapped, he was on his guard against this man for himself and his friends. So now, while the struggle between the two men was going on, George was standing with his rifle ready for use. He saw the flash of the knife, the descending stroke, and knowing the design, made his rifle speak, only a moment too late to save Long Tom. The bullet sped on its way and penetrated the brain of the dwarf, and the two men fell to the ground locked in each other's arms.

In the meantime a crowd had surrounded Sam Wiles, who had backed up against a giant oak tree and stood holding his rifle by its barrel, determined to sell his life as dearly as possible. Again Jasper Very became his good angel. In a firm voice he pleaded with his companions not to redden their hands with a fellow creature's blood.

However, some resisted his plea. One planter cried: "You saved his worthless life once before and said the law would punish him. How has he been punished! By shooting down some of our best neighbors. I say a bullet ought to let daylight through his onery carcass, and I'll be the one to fire it." With this remark he raised his gun to his shoulder and pulled the trigger; but before the weapon went off Jasper knocked the barrel up in the air, and the lead went flying among the leaves.

"Man, that was a reckless and cowardly act," expostulated Very. "It is true Wiles escaped from prison, but he will not do so again. He will be more closely guarded, and if he is found guilty of murder, will be properly punished." Then, turning to Wiles, he said: "You see, Wiles, resistance is useless, and by showing it you will throw your life away. Surely you are not ready for death, and I beseech you to lay down your rifle and submit to be made a prisoner."

Life is sweet, even to ruffians at bay, and Wiles, changing his decision, made with Turner not to be taken alive, said: "If you fellers will not hurt me, I'll put myself in yer hands." The crowd consenting, Jasper Very promised that no harm should be done him, and then Wiles threw down his weapon and a constable placed handcuffs upon him.

In the fighting Wiles and Turner had become separated more than a hundred feet, so that the crowd which arrested Wiles did not know of the tragedy by the other tree. When they came up with their prisoner, they saw the two men lying in the shade of an oak. Some one had thrown a coat over Turner's body.

Edward T. Curnick

When Jasper Very looked upon Long Tom, he knew that death was near. His eyes were becoming glassy and his sallow cheeks were of an ashen hue. That mysterious shadow thrown by the wings of the approaching death angel settled on his face. John Larkin was kneeling over him, trying to administer what ease and comfort he could. He was suffering great pain, but he bore it with utmost patience. Jasper Very was greatly moved at the sight. Kneeling by his side, he took his knotted and powerful hand in one of his and rubbed it gently with the other. Tears came to his eyes as he saw this rough but reclaimed moonshiner in his last agony.

The sufferer spoke, and his naturally slow speech was slower still; "Good-by, cumrades, I'm goin' home. Long Tom has lived a wicked life; but God is merciful, an' he has put away all my sins. I ax pardon of all I hev hurt, an' forgive ary who has harmed me." Then his mind began to wander, and he thought himself in the church where he had found peace in his soul. "You'uns is right, Preacher Very, whisky makin', sellin' an' drinkin' is wrong; and I'll quit it for good frum dis night on. O dat sweet music, how good it makes me feel!

'Jesus, Lover of my soul,
Let me to thy bosom fly.
Safe into the haven guide,
O receive my soul at last.'

"Hush! Dey air singin' ag'in, an' how her sweet voice leads all de rest:

'Other—refuge—have—I—none;
Hangs—my—helpless—soul—on—thee.'

"Dat—is—my—prayer—my—only—hope. Long—Tom will—go—home—home—to—God—on—dat—prayer."

He straightened his tall form on the grassy slope under the kindly shadow of the mighty oak. A look of peace and pure content came into his face, as though he were glad to have his discharge; he gave one look through the leafy top of the tree, as if beholding some form in the upper air, then slowly closed his eyes. A shiver ran through his frame, a gargle in his throat, a gasp from his lips, and all was over.

In low reverent tones John Larkin said: "Blessed are the dead which die in the Lord."

Again the captain of the moonshiners, Sam Wiles, was taken to the county jail. This time he did not escape. In process of time he and the other prisoners were tried for the illicit distilling of whisky, were found guilty, and sentenced to the penitentiary at Frankfort for a term of years. The charge of murder was not pressed against them. So they pass from this history.

Edward T. Curnick

CHAPTER XXIV

"I THEE WED"

The golden month of September saw Viola much improved in health. Her wound had healed nicely, thanks to her strong constitution and to the care she had received from the physician and nurse. Now she was rapidly convalescing, and as the fine autumn days went by she was able to ride in her carriage, and even visit the mission school, though unable to teach her class of girls.

By Christmas time the roses had indeed reappeared in her cheeks, and her step was almost as elastic as ever. June found her fully restored to health. This month was to be forever memorable to her, for her wedding to Jasper Very was set for the eighteenth day.

The whole plantation was in a fever of excitement quite a while before the event was to transpire. All was bustle and commotion. Every one seemed to have a personal interest in the affair. The slaves talked and sang about it as they worked in the fields, and renewed the gossip in the evening around their cabin doors.

Aunt Nancy, the cook, attired in a dress spotlessly clean, a bright red bandanna tied around her head, was more pompous and dictatorial than ever. Her helpers had been increased for the event, and she issued her commands with a force which would have done credit to a skipper on a quarter-deck. Often she scolded those around her, but her anger was more apparent than real, and while she smote right and left with one hand, with the other soon after she patted and petted the object of her wrath.

To her children: "You, Dick and Jim, git away frum under my feet. If yo' little niggers don't cl'ar out frum dis room, ah'll beat yer wooly heads togedder. How kin Ah see dat dis cake gits jest de right brown, if yo' keep askin' me fer cookies an' things! Take dat—boxing their ears—an' march out doors."

The boys ducked a second blow, and rushing into the yard, each turned a somersault, and grinned the content he felt. Then they began to sing:

"O Miss Lu! sugar in 'er shoe,
Show me de hole whar de hog jump fru."

For days the preparations for the marriage feast went on. Such baking, boiling, and every form of cooking, was never seen in "Mount Pisgah" before.

Judge and Madam LeMonde had many things to occupy hand and brain, but still they gave much thought to the time when they should be parted from their only daughter. She and George were the idols of their hearts. To lose one from the home even to gain a preacher-son was an experience bringing pain and sorrow. Still their judgment confirmed the step; for, if they were to have the sadness of separation, they were to have the deep satisfaction of giving their daughter to a greater service.

Edward T. Curnick

Miss Viola was busy most of the time preparing her trousseau. Many of the garments were made to order in Lexington, but much fancy work on delicate fabrics was done by the bride-to-be.

The great day dawned at last. A holiday had been given to all the slaves on the plantation. The Judge decided to spare no expense in making the occasion as pleasant as possible. He had instructed his black people to have a barbecue at their quarters. Some of our readers are benighted as to the meaning of that great word. How shall we enlighten their ignorance? Words are insufficient to set forth the joy and glory of this feast. We may try our best, but much must be left unrecorded.

Two very long wooden tables were stretched on the ground behind the slaves' cabins, under the splendid natural forest trees which Kentucky boasted. The day before an ox was killed, and a deep pit dug in the ground. Early on the eighteenth, the ox was suspended in this hole and a great fire lighted under the carcass. There for hours the body roasted in its own fat. Besides the ox, succulent roasting pigs were cooked whole, chickens were prepared in various ways. All vegetables common to the season were gotten ready in unlimited abundance. Bread enough for all and much to spare appeared on the tables. Pies and cakes of many kinds lay in beautiful companionship with the other good things. Steaming coffee in abundance for all was on hand. And plenty of "Adam's ale"—pure spring water.

This barbecue feast was to be eaten after the marriage ceremony was performed.

The wedding feast for the white folks was spread on tables which had been placed under the pine trees some distance east of the great mansion. It was impossible to accommodate all the invited guests in the dining-room of the house, and Viola decided to have the dinner served in the open air under the trees. As to the quality and quantity of this feast it is only necessary to say that Aunt Dinah and her satellites had been preparing it for days, and the proud cook was intending to stake her reputation as to ability on it for all time to come. The result was worthy of the effort she had made.

On the morning of the eighteenth came the great event. Let us try to picture the scene. It was to be an open air wedding. Viola had requested that all the colored people be permitted to witness the ceremony. There were hundreds of them, big and little, old and young. They were disposed by Mose and others under the pine trees nearest to the river.

Grouped nearer to the mansion were the members of the mission school, many planters and their families, some guests from Lexington and other places. Just by the pavement in front of the piazza a chair had been provided for Madam LeMonde.

The principals in the ceremony were in a bedroom upstairs.

And now the strains of a wedding march floats out over the great company, played by a pianist from Paducah.

With slow and measured step the wedding party descend the broad stairway. We see Susanna Spink walking before. In her hand is a basket of magnificent roses. These with leaves of others she strews in the way before the approaching persons.

First come George LeMonde, best man, and Miss Stella Nebeker, bridesmaid, with her arm linked in his. Then follow arm in arm Rev. Jasper Very, bridegroom, and Rev. John Larkin, the officiating minister. In the rear we behold the lovely bride, Miss Viola LeMonde, beautifully dressed, leaning upon the arm of her father, Judge LeMonde. Under the shadow of the pine trees, near the piazza, the wedding company take position, and the ceremony begins.

The minister asks: "Who gives the bride away?" The Judge replies: "I give the bride away," and he walks to the rear while the bride steps to the side of the bridegroom. The ceremony, brief but most impressive, is conducted according to the ritual of the church, and the minister solemnly pronounces them husband and wife.

Presently the black people under the leadership of Mose and others go to their quarters to enjoy the great barbecue feast. The white people are invited to take seats around the loaded tables placed under the pines trees. As we glance over the company we behold many kind friends whom we have met in the course of this narrative. A large number from the mission school were there, including the whole Spink family, and some members of the Sneath and Wiles families. They were under the care of Miss Henrietta Harvey, who was now their capable and devoted superintendent.

Jolly Costello Nebeker and his good lady were present. He seemed to thrive in every way by running his tavern on cold water principles. His hearty, hilarious laugh was as contagious as the measles. Honest David Hester and his folks were given seats near the head of the table. The other planters were also well represented: Abner Hunt, the fiery little man from down river, and Hans Schmidt, the large, fair-faced German, with several others. Hiram Sanders, the herculean blacksmith of Bridgewater, had a place at the table.

When the great feast was nearly over and ices were being served, Judge LeMonde arose and thus spoke: "Dear friends, I do not wish to interrupt the meal, neither do I wish to make a speech, only to say that Madam LeMonde and myself count this one of the greatest days of our lives. It surely has a tinge of sorrow in it but the joy far surpasses the sadness. I am very glad indeed to behold you enjoying the felicities of the occasion. There is a bit of the program to take place that nobody on the grounds knows anything about except Mrs. LeMonde and myself. I request at this time that my son George go to the slaves' gathering and bring back with him my servant Mose."

Without a moment's hesitation George started to do the errand his father asked. By the time the ices had disappeared the white man and the black man came on to the lawn. A look of curiosity and wonder passed over the company, and all gazed in the direction of the Judge and his servant.

As to Mose he was much taken aback. He appeared confused and bewildered. He thought it was not possible that his master would blame him for neglecting some duty or doing a bad deed on such a day and before such a company.

The Judge, calling his servant to come near, arose and said: "I have decided on this memorable occasion to repay in some measure the devotion and sacrifice of a very faithful and trustworthy servant. I have found Mose honest, obedient, kind, and always willing to do his part of the work. More than this he has risked his life to protect his young mistress from falling into the hands of desperate outlaws. Because of this heroic endeavor I have decided, Mose, to set you free. I hold in my hand the paper properly made out, and from this hour you are free to go where you will. But we do not want to lose you from the plantation. If you stay, I will pay you suitable wages for your work. I will also give you three acres of good land near the negroes' quarters and will build a nice frame house upon it. I am sure my daughter Viola will be glad to furnish the house as a reward for the service you

Edward T. Curnick

rendered her. In due time you can bring the young woman to whom you are engaged to the house as your bride.

"What do you say, Mose, will you go or stay?"

The poor black man was almost too overcome with emotion to answer a word. Tears streamed down his cheeks, and he could scarcely stand. However, he managed to say: "Mas'r LeMonde, how kin Ah thank you fur yo' kindness! Leave you an' dis plantation? Not while de sun shines in de heavens. As Ah was willin' to die fer Miss Viola, I would any time lay dow my life fer you, Judge, or ary one of de fambly."

"Well, you are a good boy, and," after handing him the paper, "now you can go to your friends at the quarters."

When the curtain was rung down on this scene, in a metaphorically sense, it rose on another of much interest.

The wedding party and guests were still sitting at the tables when honest David Hester, arising to his feet, said: "I move that we all drink a toast to our newly married friends, and that we drink it in pure cold water. Also, that John Larkin speak to the toast in behalf of the company." This motion was seconded by more than a dozen voices, the glasses were filled from the living spring, and the toast was drunk in the best liquid the world has ever seen.

John Larkin arose and said: "It gives me great pleasure to speak a few words on this happy and auspicious occasion. First, I wish to thank Judge and Madam LeMonde for the sumptuous repast they have provided for all who are present. (Loud applause all down the line.) Next, I desire to say some true words respecting our honored bridegroom. I have known Jasper Very for several years, and have been his colleague most of the time. I do not overstep the mark when I declare that he is the greatest preacher in Kentucky today. (Cries of "That's so," and applause.) He stands foursquare for righteousness seven days in the week. He is a terror to evil doers. It is by such men's work and sacrifices that we shall stamp out ruffianism, and lift our State to a high respect for law and order. (Clapping of hands.) His career is yet before him, and I believe his name will be handed down to coming generations as an eloquent, zealous, fearless, and successful preacher of the gospel. (Loud applause by the whole company.) My only ambition is that I may be his traveling companion in the ministry as long as possible, for he is to me an inspiration, a help, and, best of all, a devoted friend. (Cheers by all.)

"What shall I say concerning the lady who this day becomes his wife? He might have searched the State over, and not found so suitable a life companion. She was the originator of the mission school, and its prosperity is seen by the number of its members who are here today. (Much hand clapping by the people from the hills.) Yes, and she would not let the fear of highwaymen keep her from the straight path of duty. By an outlaw's bullet, she was brought to the verge of death, but God in mercy spared her in answer to our prayers. God surely intended her to be a preacher's wife. He gave her a voice to sing which melts the stony heart, he gave the opportunity for culture so that she can lift up the minds as well as the morals of the people. Her graciousness is surpassed only by her humility, and her beauty of face and form only by the loveliness and perfection of her spirit. To high and low she is the finest type of American woman-hood." (Long continued applause, especially by the hill crowd.)

The after-dinner speeches were ended, and the bride and groom retired to their dressing-rooms in the mansion, where

Edward T. Curnick

the wedding garments were taken off and traveling suits substituted. Soon they appeared on the front piazza, most of the invited guests still remaining on the lawn.

By a previous arrangement Mose was to be the honored driver of the carriage, to take them to the railway station. Never was there a prouder or happier negro. He showed the importance of his duty in every turn of his body. He was dressed in a new suit of clothes, and a tall silk hat orna-mented his woolly head. He held his whip and lines like a master of horse.

Some fond good-byes, a few tears like April showers with the sun shining, a crack of the whip, and Velox and Prince are off on the happy journey.

So we leave them as with

"Two souls with but a single thought,
Two hearts to beat as one,"

they set out on their life work.

"We have heard that our hero became a mighty preacher, whose praise was in all the churches. His fields of labor widened with the years. His reputation went before him, and he was known in many States as an original and marvelous genius, but to us he will ever be remembered as The Kentucky Ranger.

Choose from Thousands of 1stWorldLibrary Classics By

A. M. Barnard
Ada Leverson
Adolphus William Ward
Aesop
Agatha Christie
Alexander Aaronsohn
Alexander Kielland
Alexandre Dumas
Alfred Gatty
Alfred Ollivant
Alice Duer Miller
Alice Turner Curtis
Alice Dunbar
Allen Chapman
Alleyne Ireland
Ambrose Bierce
Amelia E. Barr
Amory H. Bradford
Andrew Lang
Andrew McFarland Davis
Andy Adams
Angela Brazil
Anna Alice Chapin
Anna Sewell
Annie Besant
Annie Hamilton Donnell
Annie Payson Call
Annie Roe Carr
Annonaymous
Anton Chekhov
Archibald Lee Fletcher
Arnold Bennett
Arthur C. Benson
Arthur Conan Doyle
Arthur M. Winfield
Arthur Ransome
Arthur Schnitzler
Arthur Train
Atticus
B.H. Baden-Powell
B. M. Bower
B. C. Chatterjee
Baroness Emmuska Orczy
Baroness Orczy
Basil King
Bayard Taylor
Ben Macomber
Bertha Muzzy Bower
Bjornstjerne Bjornson

Booth Tarkington
Boyd Cable
Bram Stoker
C. Collodi
C. E. Orr
C. M. Ingleby
Carolyn Wells
Catherine Parr Traill
Charles A. Eastman
Charles Amory Beach
Charles Dickens
Charles Dudley Warner
Charles Farrar Browne
Charles Ives
Charles Kingsley
Charles Klein
Charles Hanson Towne
Charles Lathrop Pack
Charles Romyn Dake
Charles Whibley
Charles Willing Beale
Charlotte M. Braeme
Charlotte M. Yonge
Charlotte Perkins Stetson
Clair W. Hayes
Clarence Day Jr.
Clarence E. Mulford
Clemence Housman
Confucius
Coningsby Dawson
Cornelis DeWitt Wilcox
Cyril Burleigh
D. H. Lawrence
Daniel Defoe
David Garnett
Dinah Craik
Don Carlos Janes
Donald Keyhoe
Dorothy Kilner
Dougan Clark
Douglas Fairbanks
E. Nesbit
E. P. Roe
E. Phillips Oppenheim
E. S. Brooks
Earl Barnes
Edgar Rice Burroughs
Edith Van Dyne
Edith Wharton

Edward Everett Hale
Edward J. O'Biren
Edward S. Ellis
Edwin L. Arnold
Eleanor Atkins
Eleanor Hallowell Abbott
Eliot Gregory
Elizabeth Gaskell
Elizabeth McCracken
Elizabeth Von Arnim
Ellem Key
Emerson Hough
Emilie F. Carlen
Emily Bronte
Emily Dickinson
Enid Bagnold
Enilor Macartney Lane
Erasmus W. Jones
Ernie Howard Pie
Ethel May Dell
Ethel Turner
Ethel Watts Mumford
Eugene Sue
Eugenie Foa
Eugene Wood
Eustace Hale Ball
Evelyn Everett-green
Everard Cotes
F. H. Cheley
F. J. Cross
F. Marion Crawford
Fannie E. Newberry
Federick Austin Ogg
Ferdinand Ossendowski
Fergus Hume
Florence A. Kilpatrick
Fremont B. Deering
Francis Bacon
Francis Darwin
Frances Hodgson Burnett
Frances Parkinson Keyes
Frank Gee Patchin
Frank Harris
Frank Jewett Mather
Frank L. Packard
Frank V. Webster
Frederic Stewart Isham
Frederick Trevor Hill
Frederick Winslow Taylor

Friedrich Kerst
Friedrich Nietzsche
Fyodor Dostoyevsky
G.A. Henty
G.K. Chesterton
Gabrielle E. Jackson
Garrett P. Serviss
Gaston Leroux
George A. Warren
George Ade
Geroge Bernard Shaw
George Cary Eggleston
George Durston
George Ebers
George Eliot
George Gissing
George MacDonald
George Meredith
George Orwell
George Sylvester Viereck
George Tucker
George W. Cable
George Wharton James
Gertrude Atherton
Gordon Casserly
Grace E. King
Grace Gallatin
Grace Greenwood
Grant Allen
Guillermo A. Sherwell
Gulielma Zollinger
Gustav Flaubert
H. A. Cody
H. B. Irving
H.C. Bailey
H. G. Wells
H. H. Munro
H. Irving Hancock
H. R. Naylor
H. Rider Haggard
H. W. C. Davis
Haldeman Julius
Hall Caine
Hamilton Wright Mabie
Hans Christian Andersen
Harold Avery
Harold McGrath
Harriet Beecher Stowe
Harry Castlemon
Harry Coghill
Harry Houidini

Hayden Carruth
Helent Hunt Jackson
Helen Nicolay
Hendrik Conscience
Hendy David Thoreau
Henri Barbusse
Henrik Ibsen
Henry Adams
Henry Ford
Henry Frost
Henry James
Henry Jones Ford
Henry Seton Merriman
Henry W Longfellow
Herbert A. Giles
Herbert Carter
Herbert N. Casson
Herman Hesse
Hildegard G. Frey
Homer
Honore De Balzac
Horace B. Day
Horace Walpole
Horatio Alger Jr.
Howard Pyle
Howard R. Garis
Hugh Lofting
Hugh Walpole
Humphry Ward
Ian Maclaren
Inez Haynes Gillmore
Irving Bacheller
Isabel Cecilia Williams
Isabel Hornibrook
Israel Abrahams
Ivan Turgenev
J.G.Austin
J. Henri Fabre
J. M. Barrie
J. M. Walsh
J. Macdonald Oxley
J. R. Miller
J. S. Fletcher
J. S. Knowles
J. Storer Clouston
J. W. Duffield
Jack London
Jacob Abbott
James Allen
James Andrews
James Baldwin

James Branch Cabell
James DeMille
James Joyce
James Lane Allen
James Lane Allen
James Oliver Curwood
James Oppenheim
James Otis
James R. Driscoll
Jane Abbott
Jane Austen
Jane L. Stewart
Janet Aldridge
Jens Peter Jacobsen
Jerome K. Jerome
Jessie Graham Flower
John Buchan
John Burroughs
John Cournos
John F. Kennedy
John Gay
John Glasworthy
John Habberton
John Joy Bell
John Kendrick Bangs
John Milton
John Philip Sousa
John Taintor Foote
Jonas Lauritz Idemil Lie
Jonathan Swift
Joseph A. Altsheler
Joseph Carey
Joseph Conrad
Joseph E. Badger Jr
Joseph Hergesheimer
Joseph Jacobs
Jules Vernes
Julian Hawthrone
Julie A Lippmann
Justin Huntly McCarthy
Kakuzo Okakura
Karle Wilson Baker
Kate Chopin
Kenneth Grahame
Kenneth McGaffey
Kate Langley Bosher
Kate Langley Bosher
Katherine Cecil Thurston
Katherine Stokes
L. A. Abbot
L. T. Meade

L. Frank Baum
Latta Griswold
Laura Dent Crane
Laura Lee Hope
Laurence Housman
Lawrence Beasley
Leo Tolstoy
Leonid Andreyev
Lewis Carroll
Lewis Sperry Chafer
Lilian Bell
Lloyd Osbourne
Louis Hughes
Louis Joseph Vance
Louis Tracy
Louisa May Alcott
Lucy Fitch Perkins
Lucy Maud Montgomery
Luther Benson
Lydia Miller Middleton
Lyndon Orr
M. Corvus
M. H. Adams
Margaret E. Sangster
Margret Howth
Margaret Vandercook
Margaret W. Hungerford
Margret Penrose
Maria Edgeworth
Maria Thompson Daviess
Mariano Azuela
Marion Polk Angellotti
Mark Overton
Mark Twain
Mary Austin
Mary Catherine Crowley
Mary Cole
Mary Hastings Bradley
Mary Roberts Rinehart
Mary Rowlandson
M. Wollstonecraft Shelley
Maud Lindsay
Max Beerbohm
Myra Kelly
Nathaniel Hawthrone
Nicolo Machiavelli
O. F. Walton
Oscar Wilde

Owen Johnson
P.G. Wodehouse
Paul and Mabel Thorne
Paul G. Tomlinson
Paul Severing
Percy Brebner
Percy Keese Fitzhugh
Peter B. Kyne
Plato
Quincy Allen
R. Derby Holmes
R. L. Stevenson
R. S. Ball
Rabindranath Tagore
Rahul Alvares
Ralph Bonehill
Ralph Henry Barbour
Ralph Victor
Ralph Waldo Emmerson
Rene Descartes
Ray Cummings
Rex Beach
Rex E. Beach
Richard Harding Davis
Richard Jefferies
Richard Le Gallienne
Robert Barr
Robert Frost
Robert Gordon Anderson
Robert L. Drake
Robert Lansing
Robert Lynd
Robert Michael Ballantyne
Robert W. Chambers
Rosa Nouchette Carey
Rudyard Kipling
Saint Augustine
Samuel B. Allison
Samuel Hopkins Adams
Sarah Bernhardt
Sarah C. Hallowell
Selma Lagerlof
Sherwood Anderson
Sigmund Freud
Standish O'Grady
Stanley Weyman
Stella Benson
Stella M. Francis

Stephen Crane
Stewart Edward White
Stijn Streuvels
Swami Abhedananda
Swami Parmananda
T. S. Ackland
T. S. Arthur
The Princess Der Ling
Thomas A. Janvier
Thomas A Kempis
Thomas Anderton
Thomas Bailey Aldrich
Thomas Bulfinch
Thomas De Quincey
Thomas Dixon
Thomas H. Huxley
Thomas Hardy
Thomas More
Thornton W. Burgess
U. S. Grant
Upton Sinclair
Valentine Williams
Various Authors
Vaughan Kester
Victor Appleton
Victor G. Durham
Victoria Cross
Virginia Woolf
Wadsworth Camp
Walter Camp
Walter Scott
Washington Irving
Wilbur Lawton
Wilkie Collins
Willa Cather
Willard F. Baker
William Dean Howells
William le Queux
W. Makepeace Thackeray
William W. Walter
William Shakespeare
Winston Churchill
Yei Theodora Ozaki
Yogi Ramacharaka
Young E. Allison
Zane Grey